Preface

France, a nation synonymous with elegance, history, and artistic expression, has long captivated the imaginations of people around the world. From its towering Eiffel Tower and sprawling vineyards of Bordeaux, to the romantic streets of Paris and the sun-soaked beaches of Provence, France offers an unparalleled blend of natural beauty, cultural richness, and intellectual legacy. This book, titled "Introduction of France", aims to present a comprehensive and engaging overview of the country's fascinating history, dynamic culture, and enduring global influence.

Throughout centuries, France has stood at the crossroads of Europe, shaping and being shaped by the events that defined the continent. It has been a cradle of revolutions, an incubator of ideas, and a beacon of innovation in fields as diverse as art, architecture, science, and fashion. Its cities are living museums, where ancient cathedrals meet modern art galleries, and its countryside holds a charm that has inspired poets, painters, and travelers for generations.

This book Introduction Of France begins by taking readers through the early history of France, from its Celtic origins and Roman rule, to the emergence of medieval monarchies and the transformative period of the French Revolution. It delves into the cultural landscape of France, covering its artistic movements, literary masterpieces, and the intellectual gatherings that defined eras, such as the famous salons of the Enlightenment.

In addition to history and culture, readers will also discover the many facets of French life today, from its world-famous cuisine and wines, to its fashion industry that continues to set global trends. Whether savoring a croissant in a Parisian café or admiring the works of Monet and Renoir in the halls of the Musée d'Orsay, each experience in France speaks to a legacy that blends beauty, thought, and craftsmanship.

More than just a geographical entity, France is an idea—an idea that champions liberty, creativity, and refinement. By offering insights into its past and present, this book hopes to provide readers with not just knowledge, but a sense of appreciation for what makes France unique.

Whether you are a student, traveler, or simply a curious mind eager to learn more about this remarkable country, "Introduction to France" will serve as a gateway into the heart and soul of a nation that has inspired the world for centuries.

Bienvenue en France! Let the journey begin.

Table of Contents

Chapter 1: Introduction of France

फ्रांस का परिचय

Présentation de la France

प्रेज़ौंन्तासियों द ल फ्रांस

French is a lovely language. It is derived from Latin. I ensure to my readers that you will learn French language very easily.

French- The Language of Love, is one of the very popular international language. French is the second most widely speaking language in the world after English. Apart from English; French is spoken in all the five continents.

Besides France, French is widely spoken in many parts of the world like Canada, Switzerland, Louisiana, Quebec, Morocco, Montreal, Tunisia, Guadeloupe, Belgium, French Guiana, Martinique, Corsica, Monaco, New Hampshire, Haiti, Laos, Luxembourg, Algeria, etc. French is also the second language in the world by the number of countries that have adopted it as an official or administrative language.

Learning such a language in this multi-cultural world, opens the gates of limitless possibilities in the realm of exploration of a new culture, education, travel, career, job and so on. As author I am pleased to share that we can now learn French which, along with those benefits, will also help develop our analytical skills, boost critical thinking, and keep our memory sharp. France, sixth commercial power attracts entrepreneurs in various sectors of activities (distribution, automobile, luxury, aeronautics, etc.), researchers and the best foreign students.
Therefore learning a foreign language and more specifically French enhances one's resume, helps to build and develop one's career in the long run, and also enriches one's personality because learning a new language helps open one's mind to a world of new cultures.

A glance at France (फ्रांस पर एक नजर) (Un coup d'œil sur la France) (अं कू दोइ सूर ला फ्रांस)

France, officially the French Republic, is a country with territory in Western Europe and several overseas regions and territories. The European, or metropolitan, area of France extends from the Mediterranean Sea to the English Channel and the North Sea, and from the Rhine to the Atlantic Ocean. Overseas France include French Guiana on the South American continent and several island territories in Atlantic, Pacific and Indian oceans.

France spans 6,43,801 square kilometres (2,48,573 square miles) and had a total population of almost 67 million people as of January 2019. The population of metropolitan France is 61.1 million. 75% of French population lives in urban areas.

It is a unitary semi-presidential republic with the capital in Paris, the country's largest city and main cultural and commercial centre. Other major cities at France are Lyon, Grenoble, Dijon, Perpignan, Orléans, Cognac, Nîmes, Châteuroux and Aix-en-provence. There are more women than men. In terms of the Human Develpoment Index, France has the second place in the world for many years.

The most popular sports are Football, Rugby, Cycling and Tennis. The most important national dailies are le Monde, le Figaro and Libération. The most important weeklies are Le Nouvel Observateur, L'Express, Le Point, Paris-Match, etc. France has more than 350 types of Cheese. Some of them are Camembert, Cantal, Roquefort and Brie.

France is situated in western Europe. The water bodies surrounding France are; to its west, the Bay of Biscay (Atlantic Ocean), to the north the English Channel and the North Sea, and the Mediterranean Sea to the south. The area of is 674,843 sq. km. of which 551,695 sq. km. are in Metropolitan France.

The neighbouring countries of Metropolitan France are Belgium, Germany, Italy, Luxembourg, Spain, Andorra, Monaco and Switzerland. Due to an effort of Jules Ferry (1881-82) the primary education became compulsory and now government schools give free and secular education. France is traditionally a Catholic country.

In 1789, the State ceased to be Catholic and remained just State and the Church. Population-wise, Islam is the second religion in France. Important TV channels of France are France 2, France 3, Arte, TF 1, M6 and Canal Plus.

There are two words for 'river' in French. Rivers flowing into the sea/ocean are called 'fleuve' and those flowing into another river are called 'rivière'. There are hundreds of rivers and tributaries in France but the main rivers are the Loire, the Seine, the Garonne, the Rhône, the Rhine and the Dordogne. The Loire, which is 1010 km long is the longest river in France.

It has several beautiful castles built along its banks. The Seine which is about 770 km long flows through Paris. They are followed by the Garonne (650 km) and the Rhone (522 km).

The Eiffel Tower is an iron lattice tower located on the Champ de Mars in Paris. It was named after the engineer Gustave Eiffel, whose company designed and built the tower. The tower was built in 1889 for the "Exposition Universelle" – the Universal Exhibition – to celebrate the 100th anniversary of the French Revolution.

The construction of the tower began on 28th January 1887. The tower was completed in 2 years, 2 months, and 5 days which was truly a techinical and architectural achievement. The height of the tower is 324 meter. Today, the Eiffel tower welcomes around 7 million visitors a year making it the most visited monument in the world with a paid entry.

The Avenue des Champs-Élysées is a street in Paris. It has been called one of 'the most beautiful avenue in the world'. With its cinemas, cafés, special shops and horse-chestnut trees. The Champs-Élysées is arguably one of the world's most famous street, and is one of the most expensive strip of real estate in the world.

Several French monuments are also on the street, including the Arc de Triomphe. The avenue runs for 1.91 km through the 8th arrondissement in northwestern Paris, from the place de la Concorde in the east, with the Obelisk of Luxor to the place Charles de Gaulle (formerly the place de l'Étoile) in the west location of the Arc de Triomphe. The Champs-Élysées ends at the Arc de Triomphe, built to honour the victories of Napoleon Bonaparte.

The French National Day is celebrated on 14th July each year. In France, it is formally called La Fête Nationale and commonly 'Le quatorze juillet' (the fourteenth of July). In some countries it is referred to as 'Bastille Day' as the French National Day commemorates the beginning of the French Revolution with the Storming of the Bastille on the 14th July 1789, as well as the Fête de la Féderation which celebrated the unity of the French people on the 14th July 1790.

A military parade is held on the morning of 14th July, on the Champs-Élysées avenue in Paris in front of the President of the Republic, French officials and foreign guests.

L'Arc de Triomphe de l'Étoile is one of the most famous monument in Paris. It stands in the centre of the place Charles de Gaulle (originally named place de l'Étoile), at the western end of the Champs-Élysées.

The Arc is located on the right bank of the Seine at the centre of twelve radiating avenues. L'Arc de Triomphe (in English; "Triumphal Arch") honours those who fought and died for France in the French Revolutionary and the Napoleonic Wars.

It was commissioned in 1806 after the victory at Austerlitz by Emperor Napoleon at the peak of his fortunes. Beneath the Arc is the Tomb of the Unknown Soidier from world war I which has the frist eternal flame which burns in memory of the dead who were never identified in the world wars. The Arc de Triomphe is a patriotic symbol as well as an historical monument.

Traditionally, it is relit every evening at 6:30 P.M. There is another feature which is greatly appreciated by visitors: a panoramic platform. Situated at the top of the monument, it offers a beautiful view of the capital, from the Louvre to the Grande Arche de la Défense. If we see any tourist guide to visit France then this is mentioned that we should go here.

e

Paris is the captial and most popular city of France. It is situated on the River Seine, in the north of the country, at the heart of the île-de-France region. Paris is a global hub of fashion and has been referred to as the "international capital of style", noted for its haute couture tailoring and its high-end boutiques. Paris is home to the association football club Paris Saint –Germain FC.

The 80,000-seat Stade de France, built for the 1998 FIFA world cup, is located in Saint-Denis. Paris hosts the annual French open Grand Slam tennis tournament on the Red clay of Roland Garros. Paris has two airports, Orly and Roissy-Charles de Gaulle.

France is oftenly called as L'hexagone because of its shape, it occupies a favorable position in the European continent between the Mediterranean Sea and the English channel. It is a country of great diversity.

Among the well-known attractions of France are its museums, its wine, its cheese and fashion. Euro (L'euro) is the currency of France. The French flag (Le drapeau français) is tricolor (blue, white and red) and July 14th (le quatorze juillet) is the Republic Day of France.

France has long been a global centre of art, science and philosophy. It hosts Europe's fourth-largest number of cultural UNESCO World Heritage Sites and receives around 83 million foreign tourists annually, the most of any country in the world.

France is a developed country with the world's sixth-largest economy by nominal GDP and ninth-largest by purchasing power parity. In terms of aggregate household wealth, it ranks fourth in the world.

France performs well in international rankings of education, health care, life expectancy, and human development. France remains a great power in the world, being one of the five permanent members of the United Nations Security Council with the power to Veto and an official nuclear-weapon state. It is a leading member state of the European Union and the Eurozone.

It is also a member of the Group of 7, North Atlantic Treaty Organization (NATO), Organisation for Economic Co-operation and Development (OECD), the World Trade Organization (WTO), and La Francophonie. It is the fourth biggest economic power and the fourth biggest exporter in the world.

It has the strongest agriculture in the whole European Union. It is on the first place among all European countries as far as the production of meat is concerned. Ten most important companies of France are:

1. ELE Aquitaine (petrol)
2. EDF (electricity)
3. Renault (automobile)
4. Peugeot-Citroën (automobile)
5. Alcatel (electronic)
6. Total (petrol)
7. Générale des eaux (mineral water)
8. France Telecom (telecommnunication)
9. Lecerc (hypermarket)
10. Carrefour (hypermarket)

Originally applied to the whole Frankish Empire, the name "France" comes from the Latin Francia, or "country of the Franks". Modern France is still named today Francia in Italian and Spanish, Frankreich in German and Frankrijk in Dutch, all of which have the same historical meaning.

There are various theories as to the origin of the name Frank. Following the precedents of Edward Gibbon and Jacob Grimm, the name of the Franks has been linked with the word frank (free) in English.

It has been suggested that the meaning of "free" was adopted because, after the conquest of Gaul, only Franks were free of taxation. Another theory is that it is derived from the Proto-Germanic word frankon, which translates as javelin or lance as the throwing axe of the Franks was known as a Francisca.

However, it has been determined that these weapons were named because of their use by the Franks, not the other way around.

In the 19th century Napoleon took power and established the first French empire, whose subsequent Napoleonic Wars shaped the course of continental Europe. Following the collapse of the empire, France endured a tumultuous succession of governments culminating with the establishment of the French Third Republic in 1870.

France was a major participant in the First World War, from which it emerged victorious, and was one of the Allied Powers in the Second World War, but came under occupation by the Axis Powers in 1940. Following liberation in 1944, a Fourth Republic was established and later dissolved in the course of the Algerian War.

The Fifth Republic, led by Charles de Gaulle, was formed in 1958 and remains to this day. Algeria and nearly all the other colonies became independent in the 1960s and typically retained close economic and military connections with France.

The European territory of France covers the largest area among European Union members. France possesses a wide variety of landscapes, from coastal plains in the north and west to mountain ranges of the Alps in the southeast, the Massif Central in the south central and Pyrenees in the southwest.

Due to its numerous overseas departments and territories scattered across the planet, France possesses the second-largest Exclusive Economic Zone (EEZ) in the world, covering 11,035,000 km^2 (4,260,000 mi^2), just behind the EEZ of the United States (11,351,000 km^2 / 4,383,000 mi^2), but ahead of the EEZ of Australia (8,148,250 km^2 / 4,111,312 mi^2). Its EEZ covers approximately 8% of the total surface of all the EEZs of the world.

At 4,810.45 metres (15,782 ft) above sea level, the highest point in Western Europe, Mont Blanc, is situated in the Alps on the French and Italian border.

France also has extensive river systems such as the Seine, the Loire, the Garonne, and the Rhone, which divides the Massif Central from the Alps and flows into the Mediterranean Sea at the Camargue.

The constitution of the Fifth Republic was approved by referendum on 28th September 1958. It greatly strengthened the authority of the executive in relation to parliament.

The executive branch itself has two leaders: the President of the Republic, who is head of state and is elected directly by universal adult suffrage for a 5-year term (formerly 7 years), and the Government, led by the president-appointed Prime Minister.

The French parliament is a bicameral legislature comprising a National Assembly and a Senate.

The National Assembly deputies represent local constituencies and are directly elected for 5-year terms. The Assembly has the power to dismiss the government, and thus the majority in the Assembly determines the choice of government.

Senators are chosen by an electoral college for 6-year terms (originally 9-year terms), and one half of the seats are submitted to election every 3 years starting in September 2008.

France uses a civil legal system; that is, law arises primarily from written statutes; judges are not to make law, but merely to interpret it (though the amount of judicial interpretation in certain areas makes it equivalent to case law).

Basic principles of the rule of law were laid in the Napoleonic Code (which was, in turn, largely based on the royal law codified under Louis XIV). In agreement with the principles of the Declaration of the Rights of Man and of the Citizen, law should only prohibit actions detrimental to society.

As Guy Canivet, first president of the Court of Cassation, wrote about the management of prisons: Freedom is the rule, and its restriction is the exception; any restriction of Freedom must be provided for by Law and must follow the principles of necessity and proportionality.

That is, Law should lay out prohibitions only if they are needed, and if the inconveniences caused by this restriction do not exceed the inconveniences that the prohibition is supposed to remedy.

French law is divided into two principal areas: private law and public law. Private law includes, in particular, civil law and criminal law. Public law includes, in particular, administrative law and constitutional law.

However, in practical terms, French law comprises three principal areas of law: civil law, criminal law, and administrative law. Criminal laws can only address the future and not the past (criminal ex post facto laws are prohibited).

While administrative law is often a subcategory of civil law in many countries, it is completely separated in France and each body of law is headed by a specific supreme court: ordinary courts (which handle criminal and civil litigation) are headed by the Court of Cassation and administrative courts are headed by the Council of State.

The railway network of France, which as of 2008 stretches 29,473 kilometres (18,314 miles) is the second most extensive in Western Europe after that of Germany. It is operated by the SNCF, and high-speed trains include the Thalys, the Eurostar and TGV, which travels at 320 km/hour in commercial use. The Eurostar, along with the Eurotunnel Shuttle, connects with the United Kingdom through the Channel Tunnel.

Rail connections exist to all other neighbouring countries in Europe, except Andorra. Intra-urban connections are also well developed with both underground services (Paris, Lyon, Lille, Marseille, Toulouse & Rennes) and tramway services (Nantes, Strasbourg, Bordeaux, Grenoble & Montpellier) complementing bus services.

While travelling in France we can take the high speed TGV that gets us to Lyon from Paris in just two hours. The TGV also links Paris to Bordeaux, Brest and Nantes. Don't forget to book a seat; it is compulsory on TGV.

Fashion has been an important industry and cultural export of France since the 17th century, and modern "haute couture" originated in Paris in the 1860s. Today, Paris, along with London, Milan, and New York City, is considered one of the world's fashion capitals, and the city is home or headquarters to many of the premier fashion houses.
The expression Haute couture is, in France, a legally protected name, guaranteeing certain quality standards.

The association of France with fashion and style dates largely to the reign of Louis XIV when the luxury goods industries in France came increasingly under royal control and the French royal court became, arguably, the arbiter of taste and style in Europe.

But France renewed its dominance of the high fashion industry in the years 1860–1960 through the establishing of the great couturier houses such as Chanel, Dior and Givenchy. The French perfume industry is world leader in its sector and is centered in the town of Grasse.

Mont Blanc or ''White Mountain'', is the highest mountain in the Alps and the European Union. It is also sometimes known as Lan Dame Blanche (French for ''the White Lady''). The mountain lies in a range called the Grandes Alpes. The two French towns which surrround Mont Blanc are Saint-Gervals-les-Bains and Chamonix in Haut-Savoie.

It was Chamonix in Haute-Savoie that was the site of the first Winter Olympics. The Mont Blanc Tunnel runs beneath the mountain between Italy and France, and is one of the major trans-Alpine transport routes. Mont Blanc massif is popular for mountaineering, hiking, skilling and snowboarding.

The Louvre Museum is one of the world's largest museums and a historic monument. It is located on the Right Bank of the Seine. It is housed in the Louvre Palace (Palace du Louvre), originally built as a fortress in the late 12th century. Remnants of the fortress are visible in the basement of the museum. The building was extended many times to form the present Louvre Palace.

In 1682, Louis XIV moved his home to live in the Palace of Versailles, leaving the Louvre primarily as a place to display the royal collection, including a collection of ancient Greek and Roman sculptures. During the French Revolution, the National Assembly ordered that the Louvre sculpture be used as a museum to display the nation's masterpieces.

The museum opened on 10th August 1793 with an exhibition of 537 paintings, the majority of the works being royal and confiscasted church property. Since 2008, the collection is divided among eight departments. Nearly 35,000 objects from prehistory to the 21st century are exhibited over an area of 60,600 square metres.

The museum also conserves brilliant works of famous artists like Renoir, Van Gogh, Delacroix and Leonardo da Vinci. The renowned painting ''Mona Lisa'' by Leonardo de Vinci is concserved in the museum. With more than 9.7 million visitors each year, the Louvre is the world's most vistied museum.

Le musée du Louvre (ल म्यूज़े दू लौवर)

In France, Christmas is a time for family reunions, gifts and candies for children, gifts for the poor, midnight mass, and the mid-night feast called ''le Réveillon''. French children put their shoes in front of the fireplace, in the hope that Father Christmas (Père Noël / Papa Noël) will fill them with gifts. The Christmas tree (sapin de Noël) is the main decoration in homes.

Another important aspect of French Christmas celebrations is the crib (crèche) filled with little figurines of saints to show the birth of Christ. It is displayed in churches and many homes. Mistletope is hung above the door during the Christmas season to bring good fortune throughout the year.

The Tour de France is the most popular and most closely followed annual sporting event held every July. A showcase for cycling, it is also a showcase for France and its landscapes. It was created by Henri Desgrange.

Today the race is organized by Amaury Sport Organisation (ASO), which at the end of the twenty stage of the Tour, presents the winner with €450,000. Henri Desgrange, decided that the leader should wear a yellow jersey.

The prestigious finish of the Tour is at the Champs Élysées, where Parisians and tourists from all over the world now crowd in, from the Place de la Concorde to the Arc de Triomphe, to see the yellow jersey arrive.

The Tour de France is an annual multiple stage bicycle race primarily held in France. The race was first organized in 1903 to increase paper sales for the magazine L'Auto.

The race has been held annually since its first edition in 1903 except for when it was stopped for the two World Wars. Traditionally, the race is held primarily in the month of July.

The modern editions of the tour de France consist of 21 day-long segments (stages) over a 23-day period and cover around 3,200 kilometres. The number of teams usually varies between 20 and 22, with nine riders in each.

France is divided into 27 administrative regions of which 22 are in mainland France and 5 regions are overseas. Each region is further divided into 2 to 8 departments. There are 96 departments in mainland France and overseas departments.

Overseas regions generally are made up of a single department. Regions have considerable power over infrastructural spending, in the fields of education, public transit, universities and research, and assistance to buisiness owners.

Some of the regions (with their capitals) are as follows:

Alsace (Strasbourg)
Burgundy (Dijon)
Ile-de-France (Paris)
Limousin (Limoges)
Rhone- Alpes (Lyon)
Brittany (Rennes) and Lorraine (Metz).
Corsica (capital : Ajaccio) has the position of a territorial collcetivity.

The Baguette is often considered as one of the symbols of French culture. A Baguette is a long, thin loaf of French bread. The word 'Baguette' means a baton or wand. The dough is generally made of wheat flour, yeast, water and common salt.

It is baked in a steam oven at over 205 degree Celsius. We can distinguish a baguette by its length and its crisp crust. A standard baguette is 2-2 ½ inches in diameter and up to 2 feet in length. Baguettes are often used to make 'subs' or 'panini'.

As part of the traditional continental breakfast in France, slices of baguette are spread with butter and jam and dunked in bowls of coffee or hot chocolate. A crêpe is a type of very thin pancake. It is made from a thin liquid batter made of flour, eggs, milk and a pinch of salt.

The batter is poured on a big circular hot plate and cooked. It is often associated with the region of Brittany in North-West France but is popular all over France.

One can see 'Crêperies' (little stalls making and selling crêpes) even in the dered sugar, bananas, nutella, fruit preserves, cheese, mushrooms, etc.

Sweet crêpes are eaten as part of breakfast or as a dessert. Camembert is a world renowned cheese produced in France. It is a soft, creamy cheese made from cow's milk.

It was first made in the late 18th century at Camembert in Normandy (in northern France).

This cheese is generally made from unpasteurized milk and is shaped into a flat, cylindrical mass weighing about 350 gram. This cheese takes about three weeks to ripen at the end of which it develops a white edible rind. The cheese is generally packed in wooden boxes and then transported.

Many of the greatest names in the perfume industry, Chanel, Cristian Dior or Estée Lauder are French, and in terms of international perfume sales,

France is leader with 30% of the world market. Catherine de Medicis, wife of King Henri II, is credited with having introduced a fashion for perfumes into France.

The real heart of the French perfume industry is actually the small town of Grasse, northwest of Nice. Grasse enjoys a mild Mediterranean climate that is particularly suited to horticulture, notably the production of Jasmine, one of the most important natural aromas used by the perfume industry.

The ''Hall of Mirrors'' is the most celebrated room in the Chateâu de Versailles. The Statue of Liberty was a figt of friendship from the people of France to the people of the United States.

On Easter, the children eat chocolate eggs. On Valentine's Day, one gives flowers to special friends. On April Fool's Day one plays tricks on another in good homour.

On Bastille Day, there are fireworks displays and parades. On 11th November, the President places a wreath on the tomb of the Unknown Soldier. The French go for a Midnight mass on the ever of Christmas.

One Epiphany, most famillies eat ''galettee'' which is a cake filled with almond paste. Epiphany is called the ''Fête des Rois''. The day after All Saints' Day, the French Cary flowers to the cemetery in respect to their loved ones who have died.

The major port of the north of France is Le Havre. The most ancient university of Paris is Sorbonne. The most modern museum of Paris is Georges Pompidou. A famous French Poet is Verlaine. Mona Lisa is known as La Joconde in French.

The painter of 'La Joconde' is Leonardo de Vinci. Le Figaro and Le Monde are French daily newspapers. Renault is a French vehicle. Hôtesse de l' air who serves people in the airplane.

The French national anthem 'La Marseillaise' was written by Rouget de Lisle. Cinematography was invented at France in year 1895. The airport at Paris is called Charles de Gaulle. A famous French painter is Monet. European Parliament is situated at Strasbourg. Excellent French wines are available at Bordeaux. M.C. Solaar is a famous French singer.

Les Miserables is written by Victor Hugo and Les Fables is written by Jean de la Fontaine. Jeanne d'Arc is a famous woman in French history. Notre Dame is the most famous church in Paris.

Alpes is famous for Skiing. Dijon is situated in the east of France. Louis Pasteur is famous personality in France. Seine river crosses Rouen. Bordeaux city is situated in western France. Patrice Loko is a French sportsperson. La bouillabaisse is a typical French dish. 1st May is workers' day celebrated in France.

Chenel N° 5 is a famous French perfume. Champs-Elysées is a famous avenue in Paris. France is a major exporter of wine. TGV is a very high speed train in France. The TGV between France and England is known as Eurostar.

Alsace is a French region. Nice city is located in southern France. France won the Football World Cup in year 1998. The Lumière brothers are inventors of French cinema. Noël is a French festival. The Alps separate France and Switzerland. Pyrénées mountains separate France and Spain. Cycling is associated with 'Tour de France'. Algeria is a francophone country.

The French National Anthem is La Marseillaise. In France, before beginning a meal, one says Bon Appétit and say Bonne Chance to someone for good luck. Pierre and Marie Curie were great French scientists who discovered Redium.

Asterix is famous French comic character. Peugeot is the brand of a French car. Air France is the national airline carrier of France. Zinedine Zindane is one of the greatest football players of the world. The French invented the Metric System.

The most popular pastime among the French is watching television followed by reading, listening music and going out with friends. The main national French newspaper for sale in a Kiosque (newsagent's stall) are Le monde, Le Figaro, Libertion and France-Soir, but there are many other regional newspaper such as Quest-Franche.

If we prefer reading weekly news magazine then we can buy L'Express, Le Point, Paris-match or Le Noveul Observateur.

The motto of France is Liberty, Equality and Fraternity. The oldest city of France is Marseille. Louvre is the most visited museum of the world. The old railway station called "Gare d'Orsay" is converted into a Museum. The President of the Republic is the chief of the State. He is elected for 5 years through direct universal suffrage.

He has special rights in case of serious crisis. He can dissolve the National Assembly. He nominates the Prime Minister. All the citizens over 18 years can vote. The 17th century in France is known as the Classical Age. The 18th century is the Age of Enlightenment.

Main political parties at France are as below:

- Parti Socialiste (PS) founded in 1971 by François Mitterrand
- Parti Communiste Français (PCF)
- Rassemblement pour la République (RPR) founded in 1976 by Jacques Chirac
- Union pour la démocratie françise (UDF)
- Front national (FN) founded in 1972 by Jean-Marie Le Pen

Important Historical years in France are as below:

800	Charlemagne became Emperor
814	Death of Charlemagne
1635	Foundation of Académie française
1643-1715	Louis XIV
1789	French Revoution
1792	The First Republic
1804	Napoléon became Emperor
1848-1852	Second Republic
1871	Commune of Paris
1875	Third Republic
1895	L'affaire Dreyfus
1905	Separation between the Church and the State
1946-1958	Fourth Republic
1958	Fifth Republic

1962 Independence of Algeria
May 1968 Student Movement

Presidents of the Fifth Republic in France are as below:

Charles de gaulle (1958-1969)
Georges Pompidou (1969 – 1974)
Valérie Giscaed d'Estaing (1974 – 1981)
François Mitterand (1981 – 1995)
Jacques Chirac (1995 – 2007)
Nicolas Sarkozy (2007 – 2017)
Emmanuel Macron (2017 – till date on 15-April-2023)

Most common abbreviations in French are as below:

SNCF : Societé nationale des chemins de fer français
CNRS : Centre national de la recherche scientifique
RATP : Regie autonome des transports Parisiens
TGV : Train à grande vitesse
RFI : Radio France International

Lesser known French inventors (कम ज्ञात फ्रांसीसी आविष्कारक) (Des inventeurs français moins connus) (देस अंवेन्तर फ्रांसे मुआं कोनू)

1. Louis Braille was blinded at three years but later invented the Braile, a reading and writing system for the blind.

2. André Marie Ampère formulated the law of electromagnetism and considered the father of electrodynamics. The base unit of electric known as Ampère is named after him.

3. Alexandre-Ferdinand Godefroy, a French hair stylist, invented the hair dryer's earliest version. It was a dome which had to be hooked up to form of heater.

4. Roland Moreno invented the memory card. Moreno diagram became the basis for the computer chip which is now used in debit cards, sim cards, mobile phones, etc.

5. René Laennec invented the stethoscope which changed how doctors diagonesd patients.

Some famous monuments at France are as below:

La Tour Eiffel (ला तुर एफेल)

La Tour Montparnasse (ल तूर मोंतपर्नास)

Le Sacré-Coeur (ल साक्रे-कर)

Le Mont Saint-Michel (ल मो सां-मिशेल)

Chapter 2: French Gastronomy

French gastronomy is known for its quality, diversity, and prestige. French gastronomy holds a revered place in the world of cuisine, renowned for its depth, diversity, and devotion to the art of cooking. It is more than just food; it is an intricate tapestry woven with history, tradition, culture, and innovation.
The art of French cooking encompasses a philosophy that celebrates quality ingredients, masterful techniques, and the joy of dining. From its humble rural roots to its elaborate haute cuisine, French gastronomy is a culinary journey that reflects the spirit of France itself.
It's characterized by a rich tradition of food and drink, and a focus on the pleasures of the table. French gastronomy is celebrated through festive meals, and is also an important part of social gatherings. French gastronomy is much more than the art of eating well; it is a profound reflection of French culture, history, and identity.
Recognized by UNESCO in 2010 as part of the "Intangible Cultural Heritage of Humanity," French gastronomy encompasses a rich tapestry of traditions, techniques, and regional specialties that have evolved over centuries. This essay explores the historical roots, regional diversity, iconic dishes, and global influence of French gastronomy, offering a comprehensive understanding of why it remains a cornerstone of culinary excellence.
France is a country of remarkable geographic and climatic diversity, and its gastronomy reflects this. Each region boasts unique culinary traditions, shaped by local ingredients, history, and cultural influences.
Provence: Known for its Mediterranean flavors, Provence offers dishes like ratatouille, bouillabaisse, and pissaladière. Olive oil, garlic, and fresh herbs such as thyme and rosemary are staples of Provençal cuisine.
Burgundy: Famous for its wine, Burgundy is also celebrated for dishes like coq au vin, boeuf bourguignon, and escargots de Bourgogne. The region's fertile land provides high-quality ingredients, including mushrooms, truffles, and mustard.
Alsace: Influenced by its proximity to Germany, Alsacc fcatures hearty dishes such as choucroute garnie, tarte flambée, and baeckeoffe. The region is also renowned for its white wines, particularly Riesling and Gewürztraminer.
Normandy: With its lush pastures and coastline, Normandy is known for dairy products like butter, cream, and cheese (including Camembert, Pont-l'Évêque, and Livarot). Seafood, particularly oysters and mussels, also plays a significant role in Norman cuisine.
Lyon: Often considered the gastronomic capital of France, Lyon offers specialties like quenelles, saucisson, and coq au vin jaune. Its cuisine reflects a blend of rustic and refined elements, drawing from both local and regional traditions.

Iconic Dishes and Techniques

French cuisine is celebrated for its iconic dishes, many of which have become symbols of culinary sophistication worldwide. These dishes often involve precise techniques and a deep understanding of flavor balance.

Soupe à l'oignon: A classic French onion soup made with caramelized onions, beef broth, and topped with crusty bread and melted cheese. It is a comforting dish that exemplifies the use of simple, quality ingredients.

Foie gras: A luxurious delicacy made from the liver of a specially fattened duck or goose. Often served as a pâté or seared, foie gras showcases the French appreciation for rich, indulgent flavors.

Croissants: These buttery, flaky pastries are a breakfast staple in France. The mastery of laminating dough with layers of butter is a testament to French baking expertise.

Ratatouille: A vegetable stew made with eggplant, zucchini, bell peppers, tomatoes, and herbs, ratatouille highlights the simplicity and freshness of Provençal cuisine.

Tarte Tatin: An upside-down caramelized apple tart, tarte Tatin is a beloved dessert that exemplifies the French knack for creating elegant yet comforting sweets.

Culinary Techniques

French culinary techniques form the foundation of many cooking schools and professional kitchens worldwide. These techniques, including braising, poaching, sautéing, and flambéing, are taught rigorously in culinary institutions such as Le Cordon Bleu. The emphasis on knife skills, sauce-making, and precise timing has made French techniques a universal benchmark in the culinary arts.

The Role of Wine and Cheese

No discussion of French gastronomy would be complete without mentioning wine and cheese, both of which are integral to French dining culture. France produces some of the world's finest wines, from the robust reds of Bordeaux to the sparkling wines of Champagne. Each region has its own wine appellations, reflecting the terroir and centuries-old winemaking traditions.

Cheese is equally revered, with over 1,000 varieties produced across the country. From the creamy Brie de Meaux to the pungent Roquefort, French cheeses offer a diverse range of flavors and textures. Cheese is often served at the end of a meal, accompanied by a glass of wine, creating a harmonious pairing that enhances both elements.

Chapter 3: The French Table: An Integral Part of French Gastronomy

The dining experience in France is not merely about the consumption of food; it is a ritualistic, cherished practice that reflects the country's deep-rooted cultural values. The French approach to meals emphasizes connection, tradition, and the art of savoring each bite.

A meal is seen as a moment to pause, relax, and engage in conversation, bringing together family and friends. Dining is as much about social interaction as it is about the food on the plate, making the French table a central element of everyday life.

Traditional French meals often consist of multiple courses, each carefully planned to create a harmonious and complete experience. The meal typically begins with an **apéritif**, a pre-meal drink intended to stimulate the appetite and set a convivial tone.

Common apéritifs include champagne, pastis, or a simple glass of white wine, often served with small nibbles such as olives or nuts. The apéritif offers a moment to unwind and prepare for the dining experience ahead.

After the apéritif, the first course, or **entrée**, is served. Unlike in Anglo-Saxon terminology, where "entrée" refers to the main course, in French cuisine, the entrée is a starter designed to whet the appetite. Popular entrées include delicate dishes like foie gras, escargots, or a simple salade verte (green salad). This course is light and sets the tone for the more substantial dishes to come.

The **plat principal**, or main course, follows the entrée. This is the heart of the meal, showcasing the culinary skill and creativity of the cook. Depending on the region and season, the main course may feature meat, poultry, or seafood, accompanied by carefully prepared vegetables and a rich sauce.

Signature dishes such as coq au vin, boeuf bourguignon, or bouillabaisse are examples of main courses that exemplify the depth and variety of French gastronomy. The flavors are balanced, with no single element overpowering the others, reflecting the French belief in harmony and finesse.

Once the main course is concluded, the **cheese course** is served. France is famous for its vast array of cheeses, with over a thousand varieties available, ranging from soft and creamy to hard and pungent.

Cheese is typically served with a fresh baguette or crackers and may be accompanied by a glass of wine. This course provides a moment to enjoy the subtle complexity of flavors and textures that cheese can offer, making it a cherished part of the dining experience.

The final course is the **dessert**, which can range from light and fruity to rich and indulgent. Classic French desserts include tarte Tatin, crème brûlée, and éclairs, each offering a sweet conclusion to the meal. Some meals may end with a small **digestif**, such as cognac or Armagnac, to aid digestion and bring the dining experience to a satisfying close.

Bread and wine are ever-present elements on the French table. Bread, usually in the form of a crusty baguette, is used to accompany nearly every course, and diners often break the bread with their hands rather than using a knife. Wine, meanwhile, is carefully chosen to complement each dish, with an understanding of pairing that reflects centuries of vinicultural tradition.

Whether it is a robust red from Bordeaux, a crisp white from the Loire Valley, or a sparkling wine from Champagne, the right wine elevates the meal, enhancing the flavors and creating a sense of balance.

Beyond the courses and pairings, the ambiance of the dining experience plays a crucial role. In France, meals are often enjoyed in a warm, inviting setting, whether at home or in a fine dining restaurant.

Attention is paid to the table setting, which typically includes a clean tablecloth, neatly arranged cutlery, and appropriate glassware for the different types of wine served. Soft lighting and a relaxed pace contribute to the overall enjoyment of the meal.

Dining in France is also marked by a sense of occasion. Even everyday meals are approached with care and respect, and special gatherings are celebrated with elaborate feasts. On holidays such as Christmas or Bastille Day, meals become grand affairs, featuring traditional dishes, festive decorations, and an extended time spent at the table.

French table etiquette further emphasizes the importance of respect and enjoyment. Diners are expected to wait until everyone is served before beginning to eat, and it is customary to keep one's hands (but not elbows) on the table during the meal. Conversations are encouraged, but they remain light and pleasant, contributing to the convivial atmosphere.

The French table is not just about sustenance; it is a symbol of a lifestyle that values balance, pleasure, and connection. By taking time to enjoy each course, appreciating the flavors, and engaging in conversation, the French create a dining experience that nourishes both body and soul.

In a fast-paced world where meals are often rushed or overlooked, the French approach serves as a reminder of the joy that can be found in the simple act of sharing food.

Chapter 4: The Evolution of Cinema and the French Film Industry

France is considered the birthplace of cinema and has had a strong film industry for many years. France has had a very strong film industry, due in part to protections afforded by the French Government. The French government has implemented various measures aimed at supporting local film production and movie theaters.

Cinema, often referred to as the seventh art, has a special place in French culture and history. France is considered the birthplace of cinema, with the Lumière brothers, Auguste and Louis, pioneering the first motion pictures in the late 19th century.

Their 1895 public screening of **"La Sortie de l'Usine Lumière à Lyon"** marked the birth of modern cinema, sparking a revolution in entertainment and visual storytelling. From this historic moment, the French film industry evolved into one of the most influential and innovative in the world, known for its artistic creativity, intellectual depth, and cultural significance.

In the early 20th century, French cinema was characterized by experimental films and avant-garde movements. Filmmakers like Georges Méliès, known for his groundbreaking film **"Le Voyage dans la Lune"** (1902), introduced fantasy, special effects, and imaginative storytelling to the medium.

His work laid the foundation for science fiction in cinema and demonstrated the potential of film as a medium of creative expression. Around the same period, other filmmakers explored realism and social commentary, establishing a balance between fantasy and reality in French cinema.

The 1930s and 1940s saw the rise of poetic realism, a movement that blended stark depictions of working-class life with a sense of fatalism and romance. Directors like Jean Renoir, with films such as **"La Grande Illusion"** (1937) and **"La Règle du Jeu"** (1939), portrayed the complexities of human relationships and class struggles, earning critical acclaim both domestically and internationally.

This era also saw the rise of notable actors like Jean Gabin, who became a symbol of the poetic realism movement. During World War II, despite Nazi occupation, French cinema persisted, producing films that subtly resisted oppression, including Marcel Carné's **"Les Enfants du Paradis"** (1945), often hailed as one of the greatest films ever made.

In the post-war era, the French film industry faced competition from Hollywood but responded with a new wave of creativity. The **French New Wave** (La Nouvelle Vague) emerged in the late 1950s and 1960s, radically transforming global cinema.

Directors such as François Truffaut, Jean-Luc Godard, Agnès Varda, and Claude Chabrol rejected traditional filmmaking conventions, embracing handheld cameras, natural lighting, improvised scripts, and on-location shooting. This movement was deeply influenced by film theory and criticism, particularly from the influential magazine *Cahiers du Cinéma*, where many New Wave directors had started their careers as critics.

Throughout the 1970s and 1980s, French cinema diversified, exploring genres such as comedy, drama, and thriller while maintaining its distinctive artistic sensibility. Directors like Bertrand Tavernier, Jacques Tati, and Louis Malle continued to push the boundaries of storytelling, often addressing social and political issues. French comedies, such as **"La Cage aux Folles"** (1978), found international success, showcasing the country's ability to blend humor with cultural critique.

The French film industry is also known for its robust support system, with government-backed initiatives like the **Centre National du Cinéma et de l'Image Animée** (CNC) providing funding and resources for filmmakers. This support ensures that French cinema retains its cultural identity while fostering innovation and creativity.

Additionally, prestigious events such as the **Cannes Film Festival** have played a pivotal role in promoting French films and filmmakers on the global stage. Cannes, established in 1946, is one of the most prestigious film festivals in the world, and its Palme d'Or award is highly coveted by filmmakers worldwide.

French cinema today continues to thrive, blending tradition with modernity. Contemporary filmmakers like Jacques Audiard, Céline Sciamma, and Michel Hazanavicius have received international acclaim for their works.

Audiard's **"Dheepan"** (2015), Sciamma's **"Portrait of a Lady on Fire"** (2019), and Hazanavicius's **"The Artist"** (2011), which won five Academy Awards including Best Picture, exemplify the enduring quality and diversity of French filmmaking. Meanwhile, actors such as Marion Cotillard, Vincent Cassel, and Léa Seydoux have become global stars, representing the excellence of French talent.

French cinema has played a vital role in the evolution of global film, from its pioneering days with the Lumière brothers to the modern era of critically acclaimed and commercially successful films. Its rich history, innovative spirit, and commitment to artistic integrity continue to make it a cornerstone of world cinema.

Whether through avant-garde experiments, poignant social dramas, or whimsical comedies, the French film industry remains a beacon of creativity and cultural expression, inspiring audiences and filmmakers around the world.

Answer the following questions. (निम्नलिखित सवालों का जवाब दें।) (Répondez aux questions suivantes.) (रर्पोंदे ओ केसचियों सुइवो।)

1. Which of the following films by Georges Méliès is considered a pioneering work in science fiction cinema?
A) Les Quatre Cents Coups
B) Le Voyage dans la Lune
C) La Grande Illusion
D) Amélie
Answer: B) Le Voyage dans la Lune

2. Which French film movement, known for breaking cinematic conventions, emerged in the late 1950s and 1960s?
A) Poetic Realism
B) French New Wave
C) Impressionist Cinema
D) Avant-Garde Cinema
Answer: B) French New Wave

3. Which of these films by Jean Renoir is often considered one of the greatest films of all time?
A) Cléo de 5 à 7
B) La Règle du Jeu
C) À Bout de Souffle
D) Les Enfants du Paradis
Answer: B) La Règle du Jeu

4. Which French director is known for the internationally acclaimed film “Amélie”?
A) Luc Besson
B) Jean-Luc Godard
C) Jean-Pierre Jeunet
D) François Truffaut
Answer: C) Jean-Pierre Jeunet

5. In which year was the Cannes Film Festival established?
A) 1929
B) 1939
C) 1946
D) 1959
Answer: C) 1946

6. What is the primary purpose of the Un Certain Regard section at the Cannes Film Festival?
A) To showcase mainstream commercial films
B) To honor the best short films
C) To highlight unique and daring works
D) To award the best animated films
Answer: C) To highlight unique and daring works

7. Which French actress, known for her roles in “La Vie en Rose” and “Inception,” has become a global icon?
A) Marion Cotillard

B) Catherine Deneuve
C) Juliette Binoche
D) Isabelle Huppert
Answer: A) Marion Cotillard

8. Who are considered the pioneers of modern cinema from France?
A) Georges Méliès and Claude Chabrol
B) François Truffaut and Jean-Luc Godard
C) Auguste and Louis Lumière
D) Jacques Tati and Louis Malle
Answer: C) Auguste and Louis Lumière

Chapter 5: The Cannes Film Festival: A Global Stage for French Cinema

A pivotal institution in the French and global film industry is the **Cannes Film Festival**, one of the world's most prestigious film festivals. Established in 1946, Cannes quickly became a symbol of cinematic excellence, drawing filmmakers, actors, critics, and cinephiles from across the globe. Held annually in the glamorous setting of the French Riviera, the festival is renowned not only for its red-carpet elegance but also for its unwavering commitment to showcasing bold, artistic, and innovative films.

The Cannes Film Festival is famous for its **Palme d'Or** award, given to the best film in competition. Winning the Palme d'Or is considered one of the highest honors in the film industry, and many recipients have gone on to achieve legendary status.

Notable Palme d'Or winners include films like **"La Dolce Vita"** by Federico Fellini, **"Pulp Fiction"** by Quentin Tarantino, and **"Parasite"** by Bong Joon-ho. French films and directors have often dominated Cannes, with works by Jean-Luc Godard, Claude Lelouch, and more recently Jacques Audiard and Julia Ducournau receiving top honors.

Beyond the main competition, Cannes features several parallel sections, such as **Un Certain Regard**, which highlights unique and daring films, and the **Director's Fortnight**, which emphasizes emerging voices in world cinema. The festival's role in discovering and promoting new talent cannot be overstated; many now-celebrated directors had their international debuts at Cannes.

Cannes is not just a film festival; it is a cultural and social phenomenon. The festival's influence extends beyond cinema, impacting fashion, media, and global discourse on art and culture. Its famous red carpet has become a symbol of glamour, while the films it screens often spark conversations about pressing social and political issues.

Additionally, Cannes has been instrumental in cementing France's position as a global hub for cinematic excellence, attracting filmmakers and audiences eager to experience the best in international cinema.

Throughout the 1970s and 1980s, French cinema diversified, exploring genres such as comedy, drama, and thriller while maintaining its distinctive artistic sensibility. Directors like Bertrand Tavernier, Jacques Tati, and Louis Malle continued to push the boundaries of storytelling, often addressing social and political issues. French comedies, such as **"La Cage aux Folles"** (1978), found international success, showcasing the country's ability to blend humor with cultural critique.

By the 1990s, a new generation of filmmakers emerged, including Luc Besson, who directed visually striking films like **"Léon: The Professional"** (1994) and **"The Fifth Element"** (1997). Besson's work, characterized by its high production values and international appeal, marked a shift towards more commercially oriented French cinema. Meanwhile, Jean-Pierre Jeunet's **"Amélie"** (2001) captured global audiences with its whimsical style and heartwarming narrative, becoming one of the most internationally recognized French films of the decade.

The French film industry is also known for its robust support system, with government-backed initiatives like the **Centre National du Cinéma et de l'Image Animée** (CNC) providing funding and

resources for filmmakers. This support ensures that French cinema retains its cultural identity while fostering innovation and creativity.
Institutions such as the Cannes Film Festival, in collaboration with these government initiatives, help maintain the delicate balance between artistic freedom and financial viability, ensuring that the French film industry remains vibrant and relevant.
French cinema today continues to thrive, blending tradition with modernity. Contemporary filmmakers like Jacques Audiard, Céline Sciamma, and Michel Hazanavicius have received international acclaim for their works.

Audiard's "Dheepan" (2015), Sciamma's "Portrait of a Lady on Fire" (2019), and Hazanavicius's "The Artist" (2011), which won five Academy Awards including Best Picture, exemplify the enduring quality and diversity of French filmmaking. Meanwhile, actors such as Marion Cotillard, Vincent Cassel, and Léa Seydoux have become global stars, representing the excellence of French talent.

In conclusion, French cinema and the Cannes Film Festival have played vital roles in shaping the global film landscape. From the pioneering days of the Lumière brothers to the present, the French film industry has continually evolved, balancing artistic innovation with commercial appeal.

Through institutions like Cannes and the continued support of filmmakers and audiences, French cinema remains a beacon of creativity, intellectual depth, and cultural influence in the ever-evolving world of cinema.

Chapter 6: France: The Fashion Capital of the World

France, often hailed as the fashion capital of the world, is a country where style, elegance, and creativity converge to shape global trends. From its historic roots in royal courts to its modern status as a hub of haute couture and luxury brands, France has maintained an unparalleled influence on the fashion industry for centuries.

Whether through timeless designs, groundbreaking innovations, or the effortless chic of everyday Parisian style, France has consistently set the standard for what it means to be fashionable.

France, and particularly Paris, has long been regarded as the **fashion capital of the world**, a title it has earned through centuries of sartorial excellence, creativity, and innovation. The country's influence on global fashion began in the 17th century under the reign of **King Louis XIV**, who promoted luxury textiles, fine tailoring, and ornate designs, making French style synonymous with opulence and refinement.

Paris soon became the epicenter of haute couture, a term that refers to high-end, custom-fitted fashion, and established itself as the leading force in shaping global trends.

The 19th and early 20th centuries saw the rise of iconic French fashion houses that continue to dominate the industry today. Designers such as **Coco Chanel**, **Christian Dior**, and **Yves Saint Laurent** revolutionized women's fashion with their timeless designs, introducing concepts that redefined elegance and femininity.

Chanel's introduction of the **little black dress** and the **Chanel suit** offered a new standard of sophistication, while Dior's **New Look** brought a post-war revival of glamour and luxury.

France is also credited with the birth of modern fashion shows and the creation of **haute couture week**, an exclusive event where luxury designers present their latest collections. Today, **Paris Fashion Week** is one of the most prestigious events in the fashion calendar, attracting designers, celebrities, and influencers from around the world.

French designers and fashion houses, including **Hermès**, **Louis Vuitton**, **Givenchy**, and **Balmain**, continue to set global trends, blending tradition with modernity.

Beyond haute couture, French fashion is celebrated for its effortlessly chic aesthetic. The concept of **"Parisian style"**—characterized by minimalism, elegance, and understated sophistication—has become a global ideal. Fashion icons such as **Brigitte Bardot**, **Catherine Deneuve**, and more recently, **Carla Bruni** and **Jeanne Damas**, have epitomized this style, inspiring countless fashion enthusiasts.

France's impact on the global fashion industry is not limited to clothing. It extends to accessories, perfume, and luxury goods. The country is home to some of the world's most renowned luxury brands, including **Cartier**, **Louboutin**, and **Chanel No. 5**, the iconic fragrance that remains a symbol of timeless allure. French craftsmanship, from leather goods to fine jewelry, is highly prized, and products bearing the label **“Made in France”** are synonymous with quality and prestige.

France is home to some of the most prestigious fashion houses in the world, each with its own unique style and legacy. **Louis Vuitton**, founded in 1854, is synonymous with luxury travel and leather goods, while **Hermès**, established in 1837, is renowned for its high-quality craftsmanship and iconic products like the Birkin and Kelly bags. **Dior**, **Chanel**, **Givenchy**, and **Saint Laurent** continue to dominate both the haute couture and ready-to-wear markets, blending traditional craftsmanship with modern innovation.

Beyond clothing, French fashion houses have expanded into accessories, perfumes, and cosmetics. Chanel’s **No. 5**, launched in 1921, remains one of the best-selling and most recognizable fragrances in the world. Similarly, **Dior’s beauty line** and **Hermès’s silk scarves** have become symbols of luxury and sophistication.

By the 18th century, Paris had become the epicenter of European fashion. Designers like **Rose Bertin**, often referred to as the first celebrated French fashion designer, dressed Queen **Marie Antoinette**, setting trends that influenced aristocratic fashion across Europe. The intricate gowns, elaborate hairstyles, and luxurious fabrics of the time cemented France's reputation as a leader in high fashion.

Chapter 7: Paris Fashion Week: A Global Event

France's influence on fashion is most visibly showcased during **Paris Fashion Week**, one of the most prestigious and influential fashion events in the world. Alongside New York, London, and Milan, Paris Fashion Week is part of the **"Big Four" fashion weeks**, but it holds a unique distinction as the most revered of them all. Established in **1973** by the **French Federation of Fashion and of Ready-to-Wear Couturiers and Fashion Designers**, the event brings together the most renowned fashion houses, emerging talents, and industry leaders for a spectacular celebration of fashion, artistry, and innovation.
Held **twice a year**, Paris Fashion Week includes two key segments: the **Spring/Summer collections**, presented in late September to early October, and the **Autumn/Winter collections**, showcased in late February to early March.
In addition to the ready-to-wear shows, Paris is also home to **Haute Couture Week**, a separate and highly exclusive event where only a select group of designers present their bespoke, handcrafted collections. This emphasis on haute couture, which Paris uniquely retains, underscores France's legacy of luxury, craftsmanship, and artistic expression.

Haute Couture: The Essence of Parisian Luxury

Unlike other fashion capitals, Paris retains a strong focus on haute couture, a term that originated in France and is legally protected. Only fashion houses that meet strict criteria—such as designing made-to-measure garments, employing highly skilled artisans, and presenting twice a year—can officially call themselves haute couture. The Chambre Syndicale de la Haute Couture, established in 1868, regulates this exclusive segment of the industry.

Haute couture collections presented during Paris Fashion Week are the pinnacle of luxury fashion. Each piece is handcrafted using the finest materials and techniques, often requiring hundreds or even thousands of hours of labor.

Designers like Elie Saab, Valentino, and Jean Paul Gaultier create breathtaking works of art that blur the line between fashion and fantasy. These shows are highly exclusive, attended by an elite audience of clients, celebrities, and fashion insiders.

The Unique Experience of Paris Fashion Week

Paris Fashion Week is not just about the runway shows—it's an immersive experience that transforms the city into a fashion playground. Iconic landmarks such as the Louvre, Eiffel Tower, Palais de Tokyo, and Tuileries Gardens serve as backdrops for many presentations, creating a seamless blend of culture, history, and modernity.

The event is characterized by a glamorous atmosphere, with streets filled with photographers capturing the best of street style, and luxury boutiques hosting exclusive parties and events.

The shows themselves are often grand spectacles. Designers go beyond presenting clothes—they create entire worlds, with elaborate sets, dramatic lighting, and live performances. From Karl Lagerfeld's iconic Chanel runway recreations of supermarkets and beaches to Dior's surreal floral installations, each show offers a unique narrative and artistic vision.

Paris Fashion Week stands as a testament to France's unparalleled influence on the world of fashion. With its unique blend of haute couture and ready-to-wear collections, prestigious designers, and emerging talent, the event not only sets the tone for future trends but also reaffirms Paris's position as the fashion capital of the world.

More than just a series of runway shows, Paris Fashion Week is a celebration of creativity, craftsmanship, and the enduring allure of French style. As it continues to evolve, embracing sustainability and innovation, it remains a beacon of elegance and a source of inspiration for fashion enthusiasts everywhere.

Chapter 8: The Origins of French Salons

The term "salon" in France originally referred to a large reception room in a private home where intellectual and cultural gatherings were held. These gatherings, popularized in the 17th and 18th centuries, were typically hosted by wealthy and educated women, known as **salonnières**, who brought together writers, artists, philosophers, and politicians to discuss art, literature, science, and societal issues.

Over time, salons became a powerful institution in French society, playing a critical role in shaping intellectual discourse, fostering the Enlightenment, and promoting the ideals that ultimately led to the French Revolution.

The origins of French salons can be traced back to **Catherine de Vivonne, Marquise de Rambouillet**, who, in the early 17th century, transformed her home into a meeting place for the elite and intellectuals of Paris.

Her salon, known as the **Chambre bleue** (Blue Room), became famous for its elegance, wit, and the high quality of its conversations. This set the template for future salons, which would blend high culture with informal discussion in an environment of intellectual stimulation.

Salons in the Age of the Enlightenment

By the 18th century, salons had become a central feature of French cultural life. This period, known as the **Age of Enlightenment**, saw the rise of intellectuals who questioned traditional authority and promoted reason, individualism, and scientific inquiry.

Salons provided an ideal platform for such ideas to flourish. Unlike universities or academies, which were dominated by men and often controlled by the Church or state, salons offered a more inclusive and independent space for free thought and debate.

Key figures of the Enlightenment, such as **Voltaire**, **Jean-Jacques Rousseau**, and **Denis Diderot**, were regular participants in salons.

Diderot, in particular, benefited from the support of salonnières like **Madame Geoffrin**, who helped fund his monumental work, the **Encyclopédie**, a comprehensive compendium of knowledge that sought to promote Enlightenment ideals. Madame Geoffrin's salon was known for its intellectual rigor and attracted some of the brightest minds of the era.

Another influential salonnière of the time was **Madame de Staël**, who played a crucial role in promoting liberal political ideas during the late 18th and early 19th centuries. Her salon attracted leading thinkers, including **Benjamin Constant** and **Johann Wolfgang von Goethe**, and became a center of resistance against Napoleonic authoritarianism.

The Role of Women in French Salons

Women played a central role in the success and influence of French salons. As hostesses, or **salonnières**, they curated the guest lists, set the tone for discussions, and ensured that conversations remained engaging and productive.

This position gave them significant social and intellectual power at a time when women were largely excluded from formal education and political life.

Notable salonnières included:

1. **Madame de Rambouillet** – Credited with establishing the first major salon in Paris, she set high standards for etiquette and intellectual discourse.
2. **Madame Geoffrin** – Known for her generosity and support of the arts and sciences, she hosted one of the most famous salons of the Enlightenment.
3. **Madame de Staël** – A key figure in political and intellectual circles, her salon became a hub for liberal thinkers and writers.
4. **Madame du Deffand** – Renowned for her sharp wit and brilliant conversations, she attracted a wide range of guests, including Voltaire and Horace Walpole.

Through their salons, these women influenced public opinion, shaped cultural trends, and provided a platform for new ideas that would shape modern France.

They bridged the gap between the intellectual elite and the aristocracy, fostering a culture of dialogue and mutual respect.

The Decline of Salons in the 19th Century

After the French Revolution and the rise of Napoleon Bonaparte, the nature of salons began to change. The political and social upheavals of the late 18th century had disrupted the traditional aristocratic society that had supported the salon culture.

Under Napoleon's rule, salons became more focused on literary and artistic discussions rather than political debate.

In the early 19th century, salons experienced a brief revival, with figures like Madame de Staël continuing to host influential gatherings. However, as formal political institutions and newspapers became more prominent, the role of salons in shaping public discourse diminished. By the mid-19th century, salons had largely been replaced by other forms of intellectual and social engagement, such as literary clubs, cafés, and public lectures.

Despite their decline, the legacy of French salons endures. They played a crucial role in the development of modern intellectual life, fostering the exchange of ideas and promoting critical thinking.

Salons helped bridge the gap between different social classes and provided a platform for marginalized voices, particularly women, to contribute to cultural and intellectual life.

Salons also had a lasting impact on the arts. Many of the greatest works of French literature, philosophy, and science were inspired or supported by the discussions that took place in salons.

The salon culture influenced the development of literary salons and intellectual circles in other parts of Europe and the Americas, spreading the values of the Enlightenment far beyond France's borders.

In modern times, the spirit of the salon lives on in various forms. Literary festivals, intellectual forums, and cultural gatherings continue to provide spaces for dialogue and debate, echoing the traditions established by French salons centuries ago.

The French salon was more than just a social gathering; it was a cultural institution that played a pivotal role in shaping the intellectual and political life of France. From their origins in the aristocratic drawing rooms of the 17th century to their influence on the Enlightenment and the French Revolution, salons provided a unique platform for the exchange of ideas and the promotion of cultural and social progress.

Chapter 9: The French Revolution

On the morning of 14 July 1789, the city of Paris was in a state of alarm. The king had commanded troops to move into the city. Rumors spread that he would soon order the army to open fire upon the citizens. Some 7,000 men and women gathered in front of the town hall and decided to form a peoples' militia. They broke into a number of government buildings in search of arms. Finally, a group of several hundred people marched towards the eastern part of the city and stormed the fortress-prison, the Bastille, where they hoped to find hoarded ammunition.

In the armed fight that followed, the commander of the Bastille was killed and the prisoners released though there were only seven of them. Yet the Bastille was hated by all, because it stood for the despotic power of the king, the fortress was demolished and it's stone fragments were sold in the markets to all those who wished to keep a souvenir of its destruction. The days that followed saw more rioting both in Paris and the countryside.

Most people were protesting against the high price of bread. Much later, when historians looked back upon this time, they saw it as the beginning of a chain of events that ultimately led to the execution of the king in France, though most people at the time did not anticipate this outcomc; how and why did is happen?

French Society During the Late Eighteenth Century

In 1774, Louis XVI of the Bourbon family of kings ascended the throne of France. He was 20 years old and married to the Austrian princess Marie Antointte. Upon his accession the new king found an empty treasure. Long years of war had drained the financial resources of France. Added to this was the cost of mainintaining an extravagant court at the immense palace of Versailles.

Under Louis XVI, France helped the thirteenth American colonies to gain their independence from the common enemy, Britain. The war added more than a billion livre to a debt that had already risen to more than two billion livre. Lender who gave the state credit, now began to charge ten percent interest on loans, so the French government was obliged to spend an increasing percentage of its budget on interest payments alone.

To meet its regular expenses, such as the cost of maintaining an army, the court, running government offices or universities, the state was forced to increase taxes. Yet even this measure would not have sufficed.

French society in the eighteenth century was divided into three estates, and only members of the third estate paid taxes. The society of estates was part of the feudal system that dated back to the middle ages. The term Old Regime is usually used to describe the society and institutions of France before 1789. System of estates in French society was organized. Peasants made up about 90 percent of the population.

However, only a small number of them owned the land they cultivated. About 60 percent of the land was owned by nobles, the Church and other richer members of the third estate. The members of the first two estastes, that is, the Clergy and the Nobility, enjoyed certain privileges by birth. The most important of these was exemption from paying taxes to the state. The nobles further enjoyed feudal privileges.

These included feudal dues, which they extraxted from the peasants. Peasants were obliged to render services to the lord – to work in his house and fields – to serve in the army or to participate in building roads.

The Church too extracted its share of taxes called tithes from the peasants, and finally, all members of the third estate had to pay taxes to the state. These included a direct tax, called Taille, and a number of indirect taxes which were levied on articles of everyday consumption like Salt or Tobacco. The burden of financing activities of the state throught taxes was borne by the third estate alone.

The population of France rose from about 23 million in 1715 to 28 million in 1789. This led to a rapid increase in the demand for foodgrains. Production of grains could not keep pace with the demand. So the price of bread which was the staple diet of the majority rose rapidly. Most workers were employed as labourers in workshops whose owner fixed their wages. But wages did not keep pace with the rise in prices. So the gap between the poor and the rich widened. Things became worse whenever drought or hail reduced the harvest. This led to a subsistence crisis, something that occurred frequently in France during Old Regime.

The Outbreak of the Revolution

Louis XVI had to increase taxes for reasons due to reasons mentioned in above paragraph but in France of the Old Regime the monarch did not have the power to impose taxes according to his will alone. Rather he had to call a meeting of the Estates General which would then pass his proposals for new taxes. The Estates General was a political body to which the three estates sent their representatives. However, the monarch alone could decide when to call a meeting of this body. The last time it was in 1614.

On 5 May 1789, Louis XVI called together an assembly of the Estates General to pass proposals for new taxes. A resplendent hall in Versailles was prepared to host the delegates. The first and second estates sent 300 representatives each, who were seated in rows facing each other on two sides, while the 600 members of the third estate had to stand at the back. The third estate was representated by its more prosperous and educated members. Peasants, artisans and women were denied entry to the assembly.

However, their grievances and demands were listed in 40,000 letters which the representatives had brought with them. Voting in the Estates General in the past had been conducted according to the principle that each estate had one vote. This time too Louis XVI was determined to continue the same practice. But members of the third estate demanded that voting now be conducted by the assembly as a whole, where each member would have one vote. This was one of the democratoic principles put forward by philosophers like Rousseau in his book *The Social Contract*. When the king rejected this proposal, members of the third estate walked out of the assembly in protest. The National Assembly completed the draft of the constitution in 1791. Its main object was to limit the powers of the monarch.

These powers instead of being concentrated in the hands of one person, were now separated and assigned to different institutions – the legislature, executive and judiciary. This made France a constitutional monarchy. The Constitution began with a Declaration of the Rights of Man and Citizen. Rights such as the right to life, freedom of speech, freedom of opinion, equality before law, were established as 'natural and inalienable' rights, that is, they belonged to each human being by birth and could not be taken away. It was the dute of the state to protect each citizen's natural rights.

France Abolishes Monarchy and Becomes a Republic

The situation in France continued to be tense during the following years. Although Louis XVI had signed the Constitution, he entered into secret negotiations with the King of Prussis. Rulers of other neighbouring countries too worried by the developments in France and made plans to send troops to put down the events that had been taking place there since the summer of 1789. Before this could happen, the National Assemebly voted in April 1792 to declare war against Prussia and Austria. Thousands of volunteers thronged from the provinces to join the army.

They saw this as a war of the people against kings and aristocracies all over Europe. Among the patriotic songs they sang was the Marseillaise, compiosed by the poet Roget de L'Isle. It was sung for the first time by volunteers from Marseilled as they marched into Paris and so got its name. The Marseillasie is now the national anthem of France. The revolutionary wars brought losses and economic difficulties to the people.

While the men were away fighting at the front, women were left to cope with the tasks of earnings living and looking after their families. Large sections of the population were convinced that the revolution had to be carried further, as the Constitution of 1791 gave political rights only to the richer sections of society.

The newly elected assembly was called the Convention. On 21 September 1792 it abolished the monarchy and declared France a republic. Louis XVI was sentenced to death by a court on the charge of treason. On 21 January 1793 he was executed publicly at the Place de la Concorde.

Did Women have a Revolution?

From the very beginning women were active participants in the events which brought about so many important changes in French society. They hoped that their involvement would pressurize the revolutionary government to introduce measures to improve their lives.

Most women of the third estate had to work for a living. They worked as seamstresses or laundresses, sold flowers, fruits and vegetables at the market, or were employed as domestic servents in the houses of prosperous people. Most women did not have access to education or job training. In order to discuss and voice their interests women started their own political clubs and newspapers. About sixty women's club came up in different French cities.

The Society of Revolutionary and Republican Women was the most famous of them. One of their main demands was that women enjoy the same political rights as men. Women were disappointed that the Constitution of 1791 reduced them to passive citizens.

They demanded the right to vote, to be elected to the Assembly and to hold political office. Only then, they felt, would their interests be represented in the new government. The example of the political activities of French women during the revolutionary years was kept alive as inspiring memory. It was finally in 1946 that women in France win the right to vote.

The Abolition of Slavery

One of the most revolutionary social reforms of the Jacobin regime was the abolition of slavery in the French colonies. The colonies in the Caribbean – Martinique, Guadeloupe and San Domingo were important suppliers of commodities such as tobacco, indigo, sugar and coffee. But the reluctance of Europeans to go and work in distant and unfamiliar lands meant a shortage of labour on the plantations.

So this was met by a triangular slave trade between Europe, Africa and the Americas. The slave trade began in the seventeenth century. French merchants sailed from the ports of Bordeaux or Nantes to the African coast, where they bought slaves from local chieftains.

Branded and shackled, the slaves were packed tightly into ships for three month long voyage across the Atlantic to the Caribbean. There they were sold to plantation owners. The exploration of slave labour made it possible to meet the growing demand in European markets for sugar, coffee and indigo.

Port cities like Bordeaux and Nantes owned their economic prosperity to the flourishing slave trade. Throughout the eighteenth century there was little criticism of slavery in France. The National Assembly held long debates about whether the rights of man should be extended to all French subjects including those in colonies. But it did not pass any laws, fearing opposition from businessmen whose incomes dependent on the slave trade.

It was finally the Convention which in 1794 legislated to free all slaves in the French overseas possessions. This, however, turned out to be a short-term measure: ten years later, Napolean reintroduced slavery. Plantation owners understood their freedom as including the right to enslave African Negries in pursuit of their economic interests. Slavery was finally abolished in French colonies in 1848.

The Revolution and Everyday Life

Can politics change the clothes people wear, the language they speak or the books they read? The years following 1789 in France saw many such changes in the lives of men, women and children. The revolutionary governments took it upon themselves to pass laws that would translate the ideals of liberty and equality into everyday practice.

One important law that came into effect soon after the storming of the Bastille in the summer of 1789 was the abolition of censorship. In the Old Regime all written material and cultural activities – books, newspapers, plays – could be published or performed only after they had been approved by the censors of the king. Now the declaration of the Rights of Man and Citizen proclaimed freedom of speech and expression to be a natural right.

Newspapers, pamphlets, books and printed pictures flooded the towns of France from where they travelled rapidly into the countryside. They all described and discussed the events and changes taking place in France. Freedom of the press also meant that opposing views of events could be expressed. Each side sought to convince the others of its position throught the medium of print. Plays, songs and festive processions attracted large numbers of people. This was one way they could grasp and identify with ideas such as liberty that political philosophers wrote about at length in texts which only a handful of educated people could read.

Chapter 10: Bastille: A Symbol of Revolution and Freedom

The Bastille, originally known as the Bastille Saint-Antoine, was a fortress in Paris built during the 14th century to defend the city from English attacks during the Hundred Years' War. Over time, it became a state prison used by French monarchs to detain political dissidents, writers, and individuals who opposed the royal authority, often without a formal trial.

By the 18th century, the Bastille had come to symbolize the oppressive nature of the monarchy and the absolute power of the king. Its dark, looming presence in the heart of Paris made it a potent emblem of tyranny, making it a target of public resentment during a period of growing social unrest in France.

The Bastille as a Prison

By the 17th century, under Cardinal Richelieu, the Bastille had transitioned into a state prison primarily for political prisoners. Writers, thinkers, and nobles who dared to criticize the monarchy or express dissent were often incarcerated there, often without trial, under a warrant known as a lettre de cachet issued directly by the king. Notable prisoners included Voltaire, who was imprisoned twice, and the enigmatic Man in the Iron Mask, whose true identity remains a mystery.

While the Bastille housed relatively few prisoners at any given time—usually fewer than ten by the late 18th century—its reputation as a site of arbitrary imprisonment and secrecy made it a focal point for public grievances against the monarchy. For ordinary citizens, it was less about the actual injustices carried out within the fortress and more about what it symbolized: the unchecked power of the king and the broader inequalities of the Ancien Régime.

Bastille Day: A National Celebration

The legacy of the Bastille is most vividly remembered in Bastille Day (La Fête Nationale), celebrated every year on July 14th. Declared a national holiday in 1880, Bastille Day commemorates the spirit of the French Revolution and the values it represents. Festivities include the military parade on the Champs-Élysées in Paris, attended by the French President and foreign dignitaries. Fireworks, concerts, and communal celebrations take place across France, symbolizing unity and pride.

While Bastille Day primarily honors the events of July 14, 1789, it also serves as a broader celebration of democracy and freedom. The day is not just about remembering the past but also about reaffirming France's commitment to liberty and justice.

The Bastille as a Revolutionary Symbol

The fall of the Bastille marked a turning point in French history, symbolizing the collapse of royal tyranny and the beginning of the French Revolution. It inspired uprisings across France, including the Great Fear (La Grande Peur), a period of widespread rural panic and revolt. The event also demonstrated the power of the common people to challenge authority, setting a precedent for popular movements in subsequent revolutions.

In the political arena, the Bastille's fall fueled the radicalization of the National Assembly, leading to significant reforms. The Declaration of the Rights of Man and of the Citizen, adopted in August 1789, codified principles of liberty, equality, and fraternity, ideals that the storming of the Bastille came to embody.

The Site of the Bastille Today

The Bastille itself no longer stands. After its destruction, the area was transformed over the years into the Place de la Bastille, a bustling square in modern-day Paris. The square features the July Column (Colonne de Juillet), erected in 1840 to honor those who died during the July Revolution of 1830, another pivotal moment in French history.

Although the physical structure is gone, remnants of the Bastille can still be found. Archaeological excavations in the 19th and 20th centuries uncovered parts of its foundation, which are displayed at the Place de la Bastille and the nearby Métro Bastille station. These artifacts serve as tangible reminders of the fortress's significance and the revolutionary zeal it inspired.

The Bastille's legacy transcends France. The storming of the Bastille has become a universal symbol of resistance against oppression, inspiring movements for freedom and democracy around the world. Its story has been recounted in literature, art, and film, ensuring its place in the global imagination as a powerful emblem of revolution and the fight for human rights.

Exercises

Exercise 1: Answer the following questions. (निम्नलिखित सवालों का जवाब दें) (Répondez aux questions suivantes.) (रपोंदे ओ केसचियों सुइवो)

Q 1. When did Louis XVI become the king of France?
(a) In 1772
(b) In 1773
(c) In 1774
(d) In 1775
Ans: c

Q 2. The book 'The Spirit of the Laws' was written by:
(a) Nepolean
(b) Montesquieu
(c) Louis
(d) Frank
Ans: b

Q 3. The eighteenth century witnessed the emergence of which new social group in France?
(a) Middle class
(b) Higher class
(c) Lower class
(d) Neighbour class
Ans: a

Q 4. An extreme situation in which the basic means of livelihood are endangered is known as:
(a) subsistence crisis
(b) struggle to survive
(c) political crisis
(d) financial crisis
Ans: a

Q 5. When did Louis XVI call an assembly of the Estate General to pass proposals for new taxes?
(a) On 5th May 1789
(b) On 5th May 1790
(c) On 5th May 1791
(d) On 5th May 1792
Ans: a

Q 6. Who is the composer of the National Anthem Marseillaise?
(a) Roget de L'Isle
(b) Austrie
(c) Jacob
(d) Nepolean
Ans: a

Q 7. Who wrote the 'Declaration of the Rights to Woman and Citizen'?
(a) Olympe de Gouges
(b) Mirabeau
(c) Frank

(d) Louis
Ans: a

Q 8. When was slavery finally abolished in the French colonies?
(a) In 1846
(b) In 1847
(c) In 1848
(d) In 1849
Ans: c

Q 9. When did French women march to Versailles and brought the king Louis XVI back with them to Paris?
(a) 5 October 1789
(b) 6 October 1789
(c) 7 October 1789
(d) 8 October 1789
Ans: a

Q 10. When did Napoleon Bonaparte crown himself as Emperor of France?
(a) In 1802
(b) In 1803
(c) In 1804
(d) In 1805
Ans: c

Q 11. The Bastille was hated by all because
(a) it stood for the despotic power of the king.
(b) it situated on a top of temple.
(c) prisoners belonged only to the Germany.
(d) Sweden was interfering to France.
Ans: a

Q 12. The word 'livres' stand for:
(a) Unit of currency in France
(b) Tax levied by State
(c) Donation amount
(d) All of the above
Ans: a

Q 13. Group of persons invested with special functions in the Church is known as:
(a) Priest
(b) Father
(c) Clergy
(d) None of the above
Ans: c

Q 14. Peasants were obliged to serve the lords by:
(a) working in his house and fields
(b) serving in the army
(c) participating in building roads

(d) All of the above
Ans: d

Exercise 2: Match the following two columns. (**निम्नलिखित दो स्तंभों का मिलान करें।**) (**Associez les deux colonnes suivantes.**) (**एसोसिये ले द कोलोन सुइवो।**)

(i) Gardens of Versailles
(ii) Statue of Liberty
(iii) Sacré Coeur
(iv) Palace of the Pope
(v) Eiffel tower
(vi) Mont Saint Michel

(a) Avignon
(b) River Couesnon
(c) Gustaver Eiffel
(d) Montmarte
(e) Libertus, the Romans Goddess
(f) Classic French Garden style

Answer: (i) (f) (ii) (e) (iii) (d) (iv) (a) (v) (c) (vi) (b)

Exercise 3: Choose the odd word. (**अलगशब्द चुनें।**) (**Choisissez le mot impair.**) (**शुआज़िस्से ल मो आपैरा।**)

(i) Louvre/Orsay/Eiffel tower
(ii) Versailles/Sacré Coeur/Louvre
(iii) Statue of Liberty/Sacre Coeur/Notre Dame
(iv) India Gate/Eiffel Tower/Notre Dame
(v) Gardens of Versailles/The Tuilleries Garden/Palace of the Pope
(vi) Basillica/Chateau/Cathedral

Answer:
(i) Eiffel tower
(ii) Sacré Coeur
(iii) Statue of Liberty
(iv) India Gate
(v) Palace of the Pope
(vi) Chateau

Exercise 4: Choose the odd word. (**अलग शब्द चुनें।**) (**Choisissez le mot impair.**) (**शुआज़िस्से ल मो आपैरा।**)

(i) Washington/Paris/Lyon/Nantes
(ii) Jura/Alps/Pyrenees/Champagne
(iii) Milk/Butter/Jam/Cream
(iv) Pâques/Noël/Fête des mères/Pentecote

Answer:
(i) Washington
(ii) Champagne
(iii) Jam

(iv) Fête des meres

Exercise 5: Match the following two columns. (निम्नलिखित दो स्तंभों का मिलान करें।) (Associez les deux colonnes suivantes.) (एसोसिये ल द कोलोन सुइवो।)

(1) Epiphany
(2) Valentine's Day
(3) Bastille Day
(4) All Saints' Day
(5) Labour Day
(6) Armistice Day

(a) November 1st
(b) July 14th
(c) November 11th
(d) February 14th
(e) January 6th
(f) May 1st

Answer: (1) (e) (2) (d) (3) (b) (4) (a) (5) (f) (6) (c)

Exercise 6: Choose the correct French word. (सही फ्रेंच शब्द चुनें।) (Choisissez le bon mot français.) (शुआज़िस्से ले बोन मो फ्रोंसे।)

(1) April Fool's Day is called:
  (a) Poisson d'avrill
  (b) Fête des pêres
  (c) Noël
  (d) Fête de la lumière

(2) Mother's Day is called :
  (a) Pâques
  (b) Assomption
  (c) Fête des pères
  (d) Fête des meres

(3) Bastille Day is called:
  (a) Noël
  (b) Toussaint
  (c) Fête Nationale
  (d) Poisson d´avrill

Answer: (1) a (2) d (3) c

Exercise 7: Choose the correct answer. (सही उत्तर का चयन करें।) (Choisissez la bonne réponse.) (शुआज़िस्से ले बोन रेपांस।)

1. Le français est la deuxième langue la plus répandue dans le monde. (ल फ्रोंसे ए ला दूजीयम लॉन्ग ला प्लूस रेपांद्यु दॉ ल मोंद।)

a. French is one of the very popular language in the world.
b. French is the language of love.
c. French is the second most widely language in the world.
d. French is the second priority language in the world.

2. Je suis heureux de partager que vous. (ज सुइ इयरोज़ द परताजे क वू।)
a. I am so sad to share with you.
b. I am pleased to share that you.
c. I am happy to see you.
d. I am happy to be with you.

3. Il y a plus de femmes que d'hommes. (इल्या प्लूस द फ़ाम क दोम।)
a. There are more men than women.
b. There are less women than men.
c. There are more women than men.
d. There are less men than women.

Ans: 1. (c) 2. (b) 3. (c)

Exercise 8: Match the following words. (निम्नलिखित शब्दों का मिलान कीजिए।) (Relies les mots suivant.) (रलिये ले मो सुअिवांता।)

French
1. Aimer (एमे)
2. Compétences (कोम्पेतोंस)
3. Vills (विल)

English
a. Skills
b. Love
c. Cities

Ans: 1. (b) 2. (a) 3. (c)

Exercise 9: (Fill in the blanks using.) (का उपयोग कर रिक्त स्थान को भरें।) (Complétez le vide en utilisant.) (कॉमप्लेतें ल विद ऑ युतीलीज़े।)
Le, Musée, Ancienne

The major port of the north of France is Le Havre. The most ancient University of Paris is Sorbonne. The most modern museum of Paris is Georges Pompidou.

Q 1: ......principal port du nord de la France est Le Havre. (..........प्रेंसीपाल पोर दू नोर द ला फ्रॉन्स ए लाव्र।)

Q 2: La plus .... Université de Paris est la Sorbonne. (ला प्लूस ....उनिवेर्सिटी द पारी ए ला सोर्बोन।)

Q 3: Le .... le plus moderne de Paris est Georges Pompidou. (ल ....ला प्लूस मोर्देन द पारी ए जॉर्जेस पोम्पीडौ।)

Ans: 1. Le, 2. Ancienne, 3. Musée

Excercise 10: Complete with. (के साथ पूरा करें।) (Complete avec.) (कॉमप्लेतें आवे।)
Le, La, Les

1. ________salle des glaces est la pièce la plus célèbre du château de Versailles. (_____साल द ग्लास ए ला पीएस ला पलुस सेलेब्र दू शातो द वेरसाई।) (The hall of Mirrors is the most famous room in the Palace of Versailles.)

2. _________musée le plus moderne de Paris est Georges Pompidou. (_______म्यूसे ला प्लुस मोर्देन द पारी ए जॉर्जेस पोम्पीडौ।) (The most modern museum in Paris is Georges Pompidou.)

3. _________Alpes séparent la France et la Suisse. (_____आल्प सेपारो ल फ्रॉन्स ए ला सुईसा।) (The Alps separate France and Switzerland.)

Ans: 1. La, 2. Le, 3. Les

Exercise 11: Dites Vrai ou Faux. (दीत व्रे उ फो।) (Write True or False.) (सही या गलत लिखें।)

Population lives in urban areas. It is a semi-presidential unitary republic whose capital is Paris, the largest city in the country and the main cultural and commercial center. Other major cities in France are Lyon, Grenoble, Dijon, Perpignan, Orleans, Cognac, Nîmes, Châteuroux and Aix-en-provence. There are more women than men. In terms of human development index, France ranks second in the world after Canada.

The most popular sports are football, rugby, cycling and tennis. The most important national dailies are Le Monde, Le Figaro and Liberation. The most important weeklies are Le Nouvel Observateur, L'Express, Le Point, Paris-Match, etc. France has more than 350 kinds of cheese. Some of them are Camembert, Cantal, Roquefort and Brie.

Translation of above paragraph in French is as below:

Population vit dans les zones urbaines. C'est une république unitaire semi-présidentielle dont la capitale est Paris, la plus grande ville du pays et le principal centre culturel et commercial. Les autres grandes villes de France sont Lyon, Grenoble, Dijon, Perpignan, Orléans, Cognac, Nîmes, Châteuroux et Aix-en-provence. Il y a plus de femmes que d'hommes. En termes d'indice de développement humain, la France occupe la deuxième place au monde après le Canada.

Les sports les plus populaires sont le football, le rugby, le cyclisme et le tennis. Les quotidiens nationaux les plus importants sont le Monde, le Figaro et Libération. Les hebdomadaires les plus importants sont Le Nouvel Observateur, L'Express, Le Point, Paris-Match, etc. La France compte plus de 350 sortes de Fromages. Certains d'entre eux sont le camembert, le cantal, le roquefort et le brie.

1. Dans la suite qu'elle ville n'est pas située en France ? (दॉ ल सुइत केल विल्ल नेपा सीतूए ओ फ्रॉन्स ?) (In the following Which city is not located in France?)
a) Dijon
b) Perpignan
c) Seville
d) Orléans

2. Quel est le sport populaire en France ? (केल ए ल स्पॉर पॉपुलेर ओ फ्रॉन्स ?) (What is the popular sport in France?)

a) Cricket
b) Basketball
c) Swimming
d) Football

3. Au terme de l'indice de développement humain, la France occupe la ______ place mondiale. (ओ तेर्म द लांदिस द देवेलोप्मो उमां, ल फ्रॉन्स ओक्यूप ला ________प्लास मोनदिआला) (At the end of the human development index, France occupies the ______ place in the world.)
a) Première (First)
b) Deuxième (Second)
c) Troisième (Third)
d) Quatrième (Fourth)

Ans: 1. (c) 2. (d) 3. (b)

Excercise 12: Chassez l'intrus. (शासे लैंत्रु ।) (Select the different.) (अलग को चुनें।)

1. a) France (France)
   b) Paris (Paris)
   c) Italie (Italy)
   d) Inde (India)

2. a) Oeufs (Eggs)
   b) Poulet (Chicken)
   c) Chocolat (Chocolate)
   d) Poisson (Fish)

3. a) Aimer (Love)
   b) Comme (Like)
   c) Détester (Hate)
   d) Beau (Beautiful)

Ans: 1. (d) 2. (c) 3. (c)

Exercise 13: Choisissez les bonnes réponses. (शुआज़िस्से ले बोन रेपांसा) (Choose the correct answers.) (सही उत्तरों का चुनाव करें।)

1. La ''Galerie des Glaces'' est la salle la plus célèbre du Château de Versailles.
ला ''गेलरी दे ग्लास'' ए ला साल ला प्लूस सेलेब्र द्यु शातो द वरसेई।
पैलेस ऑफ वर्साय में "गैलरी डेस ग्लासेस" सबसे प्रसिद्ध कमरा है।
"Hall of Mirrors'' is the most famous room in the Chateau du Versailles.
"Hall of Mirrors" was the most famous room in the Chateau de Versailles.
"Hall of Mirrors" are the most famous room in the Chateau de Versailles.
The ''Hall of Mirrors'' is the most famous room in the Chateau de Versailles.

2. À Pâques, les enfants mangent des œufs en chocolat.
अ पाक्, ले जोफों मोंज़ देज़फ़ अं शोकोला।
ईस्टर पर बच्चे चॉकलेट अंडे खाते हैं।
The children eat chocolates and banana on Easter.

The children are eating chocolates.
The child eats chocolates and eggs on Easter.
On Easter, the children eat chocolate eggs.

3. Le jour de la Bastille, il y a des feux d'artifice et des défilés.
ल ज़ूर द ला बास्तील, इलया दे फ दार्तीफीस ए दे देफिले।
बैस्टिल दिवस पर आतिशबाजी और परेड होती है।
There are fireworks displays on Bastille days.
Fireworks are displays on Bastille days.
On Bastille Day, there are fireworks displays and parades.
Fireworks displays on Bastille days.

4. Le port principal du nord de la France est Le Havre.
ल पोर्त प्रिंसिपाल द्यु नोर्द द ला फ्रांस ए ल हाव्र।
उत्तरी फ्रांस का मुख्य बंदरगाह ले हावरे है।
The major port of the north of France is Le Havre.
Le Havre is the minor port of north France.
Major port of south France is Le Havre.
The principal port of new France is.

5. La plus ancienne université de Paris est la Sorbonne.
ला प्लूस आनिसिएन युनिवर्सिते द पारी ए ला सोरबोन्न।
पेरिस का सबसे पुराना विश्वविद्यालय सोरबोन है।
Sorbonne is the famous University in Paris.
The most ancient University of Paris is Sorbonne.
Paris's University Sorbonne is the most famous University.
Sorbonne the famous University in Paris.

6. Mona Lisa est connue sous le nom de La Joconde en français. Le peintre de "La Joconde" est Léonard de Vinci.
मोना लीशा ए कोन्यु सू ल नो द ला ज़कोंद अं फ्रांसे। ल पिएन्त्र द "ला ज़कोंद" ए लेओनार्द द विंसी।
मोनालिसा को फ्रेंच में ला जोकोंडे के नाम से जाना जाता है। "ला जोकोंडे" के चित्रकार लियोनार्डो दा विंची हैं।
Mona Lisa is known as La Joconde in French. The painter of "La Joconde" is Leonardo de Vinci.
The painter of 'La Joconde' is Leonardo de Vinci.
Mona Lisa is the famous painting made by Leonardo de Vinci.
'La Joconde' is the famous painting in France.

7. Le Figaro et Le Monde sont des quotidiens français. Renault est un véhicule français.
ल फिगारो ए ल मोंद सों दे कोतिदियाँ फ्रांसे। रनो ए तां वेइक्युल फ्रौंसे।
ले फिगारो और ले मोंडे फ्रांसीसी दैनिक समाचार पत्र हैं। रेनॉल्ट एक फ्रांसीसी वाहन है।
Le Figaro is the daily newspaper of France. Renault is a French vehicle.
Le Figaro and Le Monde are French daily newspapers. Renault is a French vehicle.
Le Figaro and Le Monde were the daily newspapers of France.
Le Figaro and L e Monde are the daily newspapers of France.

8. L'hymne national français "La Marseillaise" a été écrit par Rouget de Lisle.
लीमेन नाश्योनाल फ्रांसे "ला मार्सेइ" अ एते एक्रि पार रूज़े द लिस्ले।
फ्रांस का राष्ट्रगान "ला मार्सिलेज" रूजेट डी लिस्ले द्वारा लिखा गया था।
La Marseillaise is written by Rouget de Lisle.

The French national anthem "La Marseillaise" was written by Rouget de Lisle.
The national anthem was written by Rouget de Lisle.
Rouget de Lisle wrote the national anthem of France.

9. La cinématographie a été inventée en France en 1895. L'aéroport de Paris s'appelle Charles de Gaulle.
ला सिनेमातोग्राफी अ एते एनवेनते अं फ्रांस अं 1895. लेरोपोर्त द पारी सापेल चार्लस द गल।
सिनेमैटोग्राफी का आविष्कार फ्रांस में 1895 में हुआ था। पेरिस हवाई अड्डे को चार्ल्स डी गॉल कहा जाता है।
Cinematography was invented at France in year 1895. The airport at Paris is called Charles de Gaulle.
Cinematography is invented in year 1895. The airport at Paris is called Charles de Gaulle.
The airport at Paris is called Charles de Gaulle.
Cinematography is invented in 1895.

10. La ville de Bordeaux est située dans l'ouest de la France. Patrice Loko est un sportif français.
ला वील द बोर्दो ए सितुए दाँ लुएस् द ला फ्रांस। पात्रीक लोको ए अं स्पोरतीफ़ फ्रांसे।
बोर्डो शहर पश्चिमी फ्रांस में स्थित है। पैट्रिस लोको एक फ्रांसीसी खिलाड़ी हैं।
Bordeaux city is situated in western France. Patrice Loko is a French sportsperson.
Patrice Loko is a French sportsperson.
Bordeaux city is not situated in France. Patrice Loko is a French sportsperson.
Bordeaux city has situated in France.

Ans: 1-d 2-d 3-c 4-a 5-b 6-a 7-b 8-b 9-a 10-a

Exercise 14: Reliez les mots suivants. (रलिये ले मो सुअिवांता) (Match the following words.) (निम्नलिखित शब्दों का मिलान कीजिए।)

FRENCH
1. La Joconde (ल ज़ोकोन्द)
2. Hôtesse (ओतैज़)
3. Hymne (इम्न)
4. Lumière (लुमिएर)
5. Musée (म्यूसे)
6. Parfum (पारफां)
7. Célèbre (स्लेब्र)
8. Régional (रेजोनाल)
9. Un journal (जुरनाल)
10. Gare (गार)
11. Défilé (देफिले)
12. Télévision (तेलेविज़ियो)

ENGLISH
a) Hostess (मालकिन)
b) Light (रोशनी)
c) Perfume (इत्र)
d) Famous (प्रसिद्ध)
e) Mona Lisa (मोना लीसा)
f) Regional (क्षेत्रीय)

g) Telivision (टेलीविजन)
h) Parade (परेड)
i) Railway Station (रेलवे स्टेशन)
j) Newspaper (समाचार पत्र)
k) Museum (संग्रहालय)
l) Anthem (गान)

Ans: 1-e 2-a 3-l 4-b 5-k 6-c 7-d 8-f 9-j 10-I 11-h 12-g

Passage based fill in the blanks.
Exercise 15: Remplir les espaces vides. (रांपलीर लेज़ैसपास वीद।) (Fill in the blanks.) (रिक्त स्थान भरें।)

La plus ancienne ville de France est Marseille. Le Louvre est le musée le plus visité du monde. L'ancienne gare ferroviaire appelée "Gare d'Orsay" est transformée en Musée. Le peintre de "La Joconde" est Léonard de Vinci La Statue de la Liberté était un cadeau d'amitié Renault est un véhicule français. Hôtesse de l'air qui sert les gens dans l'avion.

La Statue de la Liberté était un cadeau d'amitié du peuple français au peuple américain. Le TGV entre la France et L'Angleterre est connu sous le nom d'Eurostar. L'Alsace est une région française. La ville de Nice est située dans le sud de la France.

ला प्लुज़ ओसीएन विल द फ्रॉन्स ए मार्सेइ। ल लून्र ए ल म्यूसे ल प्लु विसीते दू मोंद। लांसिएन गैर फेरोविएर आपले "गैर दोर्से" ए त्रांसफोरमे ऑ म्यूसे। ल पांत्र द "ल ज़्रोकोन्द" ए लेओनार द वांसी ला सताच्यु द ला लिबर्ते एते अं कादो दामितिए रनो एत अं वैक्यूल फ्रोंसे। ओतेस द लेर की सेर ले जेन दां लविओ। ला सताच्यु द ला लिबर्ते एते अं कादो दामितिए दू पप्ल फ्रोंसे ओ पप्ल अमेरिकेन। ल ते जे वे ओंत्र ला फ्रॉन्स ए लोंगलेतेर ए कोनू सू ल नो दोरोस्ता। लालसा एत इयुन रेज़ों फ्रांसेस। ला विल द नीस ए सितुए दां ल सूद द ला फ्रॉन्स।

The oldest city in France is Marseille. The Louvre is the most visited museum in the world. The old railway station called "Gare d'Orsay" is transformed into a museum. The painter of "The Mona Lisa" is Leonardo da Vinci. The Statue of Liberty was a gift of friendship Renault is a French vehicle. Stewardess serving people on the plane. The Statue of Liberty was a gift of friendship from the French people to the American people. The TGV between France and England is known as Eurostar. Alsace is a French region. The city of Nice is located in the south of France.

फ्रांस का सबसे पुराना शहर मार्सिले है। लौवर दुनिया का सबसे अधिक देखा जाने वाला संग्रहालय है। "गारे डी'ऑर्से" नामक पुराने रेलवे स्टेशन को एक संग्रहालय में बदल दिया गया है। "द मोना लिसा" के चित्रकार लियोनार्डो दा विंची हैं। स्टैच्यू ऑफ लिबर्टी दोस्ती का एक उपहार था। रेनॉल्ट एक फ्रांसीसी वाहन है। विमान में लोगों की सेवा करती परिचारिका। स्टैच्यू ऑफ लिबर्टी फ्रांसीसी लोगों की ओर से अमेरिकी लोगों को दोस्ती का उपहार था। फ्रांस और इंग्लैंड के बीच TGV को यूरोस्टार के नाम से जाना जाता है। अलसैस एक फ्रांसीसी क्षेत्र है। नीस शहर फ्रांस के दक्षिण में स्थित है।

1. La plus …………………. ville de France est Marseille. (ल प्लुस…………… विल द फ्रॉन्स ए मार्सेई।)

2. Le peintre de ……………………… Est Léonard de Vinci. (ल पांथ्र द …………….ए लोनार्द दे वांसी।)

3. Renault est un………………….français. (रेनॉल ए अं…………… फ्रोंसे।)

4. La Statue de la Liberté était un cadeau…………………. (ल स्तेचू द ला लिबेर्ते एते आं कादो…………..।)

5. L'ancienne gare ferroviaire appelée ………………………est transformée en Musée. (लोनसीएन गैर फेर्रोविएर आपले …………….. ए त्रांस्फोरमे ओं म्यूसे।)

6. …………………de l'air qui sert les gens dans l'avion. (…………….द लेर कि सैर ल ज़न दॉ लाविओ।)

7. ………………….est le musée le plus visité du monde. (……………….ए ल म्यूसे ल प्लुस विजिते दू मोंद।)

8. Le TGV entre la France et l'Angleterre est connu sous le nom ……………………..(ल ते जे वे ओंतर ल फ्रॉन्स ए लोंगलेतेर ए कोनू सूस ल नो…………………..।)

9. La ville de Nice est située dans le ……………….de la France. (ल विल द निस ए सीतूए दॉ ल …………… द ला फ्रॉन्स।)

10. L'Alsace est une ………………. française. (लालसा सेत युन …………… फ्रॉन्सेस।)

Ans : 1- ancienne (ancient) (प्राचीन)
2- La Joconde (The Mona Lisa) (मोनालिसा)
3- Véhicule (vehicle) (वाहन)
4- d'amitié (of friendship) (दोस्ती का)
5- Gare d'Orsay (Orsay Station) (ओरसे स्टेशन)
6- Hôtesse (Hostess) (मालकिन)
7- Le Louvre (Le Louvre) (लूवर संग्रहालय)
8- Eurostar (Eurostar) (यूरोस्टार)
9- sud (South) (दक्षिण)
10- région (region) (क्षेत्र)

Grammatical fill in the blanks.
Exercise 16: Compléte avec. (कॉमप्लेर्ते आवेक।) (Complete with.) (के साथ पूरा करें।) de, des, d'

1. Le passe-temps le plus populaire chez les Français est ………… regarder la télévision. (ल पास-तौ ल प्लूस पॉपुलेर शे ल फ्रांसेज़ ए…………….. रेगार्दे ला तेलेविज़ियो।)

2. Si on préfère lire l'hebdomadaire …........information alors on peut acheter L'Express. (सी ओं प्रेफेर लीर लेब्दोमादेर …………………आर्फॉर्मासियो आलोर ओं प आशेत लेक्सपर्स।)

3. La plus ancienne ville …………… France est Marseille. (ल प्लूस आंसिएन विल………….. फ्रॉन्स ए मार्सेई।)

4. Tous les citoyens ……………..plus de 18 ans peuvent voter. (तू ल सीतोइया ………………प्लूस द 18 ऑ प्व वोते।)

5. Le 18e siècle est le siècle………….. Lumières. (ल 18एम सीएकल ए ल सीएकल……………… लुमिएर।)

6. Les montagnes ………………Pyrénées séparent la France et l'Espagne. (ले मोंताने …………….पिरेने सेपारे ल फ्रॉन्स ए लेस्पाने।)

7. Zinedine Zindane est l'un ………………….plus grands joueurs de football du monde. (जिनेदिन जिनदान ए लां …………प्लुस ग्रोंद ज़ुएर द फुतबोल दू मोंद।)

8. Air France est la compagnie aérienne nationale………………la France. (एर फ्रॉन्स ए ल कोम्पनिये एरिने नेसियोनाल………… ल फ्रॉन्स।)

9. Le TGV entre la France et l'Angleterre est connu sous le nom …………..Eurostar. (ल ते जे वे ओंतर ल फ्रॉन्स ए लोंगलेतेर ए कोनू सूस ल नो…………… अरोस्ता I)

10. Astérix est un célèbre personnage ……………..bande dessinée français. (एस्ट्रिक्स ए अं सेलेब्र पर्सोनाज़ ………………बांद देसिने फ्रांसेस।)

Ans :1-de 2-d' 3-de 4-de 5-des 6-des 7-des 8-de 9-d' 10-de

Exercise 17: Vrai/Faux (व्रे/फो) (True/False) (सही/गलत)

1. Mona Lisa est connue sous le nom de La Joconde en français. Vrai/Faux
मोना लीशा ए कोन्यु सू ल नो द ला ज़कोंद अं फ्रांसे। व्रे/फो

Mona Lisa is known as La Joconde in French. True/False
मोनालिसा को फ्रेंच में ला जोकोंडे के नाम से जाना जाता है। सही/ग़लत

2. La Sorbonne est la célèbre université de Paris. Vrai/Faux
ला सोरबोन्न ए ला सेलेब्र यूनीवर्सिते द पारी। व्रे/फो

The Sorbonne is the famous university in Paris.True/False
सोरबोन पेरिस का प्रसिद्ध विश्वविद्यालय है। सही/ग़लत

3. Patrice Loko est un sportif indien. Vrai/Faux
पात्रीक लोको एतां स्पोर्तीफ़ एंदियां। व्रे/फो

Patrice Loko is an Indian sportsman. True/False
पैट्रिस लोको एक भारतीय खिलाड़ी हैं। सही/ग़लत

4. L'Alsace est une région française. Vrai/Faux
ललसास एत्युन रेज़ियों फ्रांसे। व्रे/फो

Alsace is a French region. True/False
अलसैस एक फ्रांसीसी क्षेत्र है। सही/ग़लत

5. La ville de Nice est située dans le nord de la France. Vrai/Faux
ला वील द नीस ए सितुए दाँ ल नोर्द द ला फ्रांस। व्रे/फो

The city of Nice is located in the north of France. True/False
नीस शहर फ्रांस के उत्तर में स्थित है। सही/ग़लत

6. La ville de Bordeaux est un pays de France. Vrai/Faux

ला वील द बोर्दो एतां पेइ द फ्रांस। व्रे/फो

The city of Bordeaux is a country of France. True/False
बोर्डो शहर फ्रांस का एक देश है। सही/ग़लत

7. La plus ancienne ville de France est Marseille. Vrai/Faux
ला प्लूस आनिसिएन वील द फ्रांस ए मार्सेइ। व्रे/फो

The oldest city in France is Marseille. True/False
फ्रांस का सबसे पुराना शहर मार्सिले है। सही/ग़लत

8. Le 18e siècle est le siècle des Lumières. Vrai/Faux
ल 18एम सिएक्ल ए ल सिएक्ल दे ल्युमिएर। व्रे/फो

The 18th century is the Age of Enlightenment. True/False
अठारहवीं शताब्दी ज्ञानोदय का युग है। सही/ग़लत

9. La cinématographie a été inventée en France en 1890. Vrai/Faux
ला सिनेमातोग्राफी अ एते एनवेन्ते अं फ्रांस अं 1890. व्रे/फो

Cinematography was invented in France in 1890. True/False
सिनेमैटोग्राफी का आविष्कार फ्रांस में 1890 में हुआ था। सही/ग़लत

10. Nice est une ville de France. Vrai/Faux
नीस ए त्युन वील द फ्रांस। व्रे/फो

Nice is a city in France. True/False
नीस फ्रांस का एक शहर है। सही/ग़लत

Ans : 1-Vrai 2-Vrai 3-Faux 4-Vrai 5-Faux 6-Faux 7-Vrai 8-Vrai 9-Faux 10-Vrai

Choose the odd one.
Exercise 18: Chassez l'intrus. (शासे लांत्रू) (Choose the odd one.) (असंगत का चयन करें।)

1. a) La France (France) (फ्रांस)
   b) Etats Unis (United states) (संयुक्त राज्य अमेरिका)
   c) Gens (People) (लोग)
   d) Grèce (Greece) (यूनान)

2. a) Le Figaro (Le Figaro) (फिगारो)
   b) L'Express (The Express) (दि एक्सप्रेस)
   c) Le Monde (The world) (ले मोंडे)
   d) L'Internet (Internet) (इंटरनेट)

3. a) Renault (Renault) (रेनॉल्ट)
   b) Audi (Audi) (ऑडी)

c) Verre (Glass) (कांच)
d) Jaguar (Jaguar) (जगुआर)

4. a) Noël (Christmas) (क्रिसमस)
b) Alphabets (Alphabets) (अक्षर)
c) Fête du Citron (Lemon Festival) (लेमन फेस्टिवल)
d) Festival du film de Cannes (Cannes Film Festival) (कान फिल्म समारोह)

5. a) Mai (May) (मई)
b) Dimanche (Sunday) (रविवार)
c) Juin (June) (जून)
d) Juillet (July) (जुलाई)

6. a) Fleurs (Flowers) (फूल)
b) Crayon (Pencil) (पेंसिल)
c) La gomme (Eraser) (रबड़)
d) Stylo (Pen) (कलम)

7. a) Ski (Skiing) (स्कीइंग)
b) Tennis (Tennis) (टेनिस)
c) Badminton (Badminton) (बैडमिंटन)
d) Ludo (Ludo) (लूडो)

8. a) Amande (Almond) (बादाम)
b) Légumes (Vegetables) (सब्जियां)
c) Raisin (Raisin) (किशमिश)
d) Noyer (Walnut) (अखरोट)

9. a) Vins (Wines) (वाइन)
b) Café (Coffee)
c) L'eau (Water) (पानी)
d) Pizza (Pizza) (पिज़्ज़ा)

10. a) Peintre (Painter) (चित्रकार)
b) Musicien (Musician) (संगीतकार)
c) Maison (House) (मकान)
d) Écrivain (Writer) (लेखक)

Ans : 1-c 2-d 3-c 4-b 5-b 6-a 7-d 8-b 9-d 10-c

Exercise 19: Choisissez la bonne réponse. (शवाज़्ीसे ला बोन रेपोसा) (Choose the correct answer.) (सही विकल्प चुनिए)

1. La France est ------------ dans l'ordre de nombres de sites du patrimoine mondial d'UNESCO. (ला फ्रांस ए ---------- दाँ लोर्द द नोंब्र द सीत द्यु पात्रीमुअन मोंदिआल द्युनेस्को।)

Première (First) (प्रथम)

Dixième (Tenth) (दसवां)

Cinquième (Fifth) (पांचवां)

Quatrième (Fourth) (चौथा)

2. La France est le membre de ----------- (ला फ्रांस ए ल मोंब्र द -----------।)

a) Union de pays de production et export de Pétrole (Union of Petroleum producing and exporting countries) (पेट्रोलियम उत्पादक और निर्यातक देशों का संघ)

b) Pays de Commonwealth (Commonwealth countries) (राष्ट्रमंडल देश)

c) Groupe 7 (Group 7) (समूह 7)

d) banque de développement Afrique (development bank of Africa)

3. Le nom « France » est arrivé par le mot « frank » de langue--------------- (ल नों « फ्रांस » ए तरीवे पार ल मों « फ्रांक » द लांग)

a) Allemand (German) (जर्मन)

b) Grec (Greek) (यूनानी)

c) Latin (Latin) (लैटिन)

d) Anglais (English) (अंग्रेज़ी)

Ans : 1-d 2-c 3-a

Exercise 20: Reliez les organisations en France avec leurs domaines. (रलिये लेज़ ऑर्गेनिसासियो ऑ फ्रांस आवे लर दोमाना) (Link organizations in France with their domains.) (फ्रांस में संगठनों को उनके डोमेन से लिंक करें।)

Organisation Domaine

1. ELF Aquitaine
2. EDF
3. Renault
4. Peugeot-Citroën
5. Alcatel
6. Total
7. Générale des eaux
8. France Telecom
9. Lecerc
10. Carrefour

a) telecommnunication
b) hypermarket
c) electricity
d) hypermarket
e) automobile
f) electronic
g) petrol
h) petrol
i) automobile

j) mineral water

Ans : 1-h 2-f 3-e 4-i 5-a 6-g 7-j 8-c 9-b 10-d

Exercise 21: Remplissez avec les mots suivants. (रोमपलीज़े आवे ल मो सुइवो।) (Fill in with the following words.) (निम्नलिखित शब्दों से भरें।)

zone économique exclusif (ज़ोन एकोनोमिक एक्सक्लुसिफ) (exclusive economic zone) (विशिष्ट आर्थिक क्षेत्र), cinquième république (सेंकिएम रेपुब्लीक) (fifth republic) (पाँचवाँ गणतंत्र), axis powers (एक्सिस पुवर्स) (axis powers) (धुरी शक्तियां), Union Européen (इयुनियो एरोपियन) (European Union) (यूरोपीय संघ), première république de France (प्रेमिएर रेपुब्लीक द फ्रॉन्स) (first republic of France) (फ्रांस का पहला गणराज्य)

1. Napolean établi le ------------- . (नेपोलियन एताब्ली ल -----------।) (Nepolean established …………….. .) (नेपोलियन ने .... स्थापित किया।)

2. Après le deuxième gère mondial la France a devenu une part de------------. (आप्रे ल दज़िएम् गेर मोंदियाल ला फ्रांस अ देवेन्यु युन पार्त द------------।) (After the second world war France became the part of ----------) (दूसरे विश्व युद्ध के बाद फ्रांस ---------- का हिस्सा बन गया।)

3. Le -----------------était établi par Charles de Gaulle. (ल-------- एते एताब्ली पार चार्ल्स द गल।) (The ----------- was established by Charles of Gaulle.) (------------ गल के चार्ल्स द्वारा स्थापित हुआ।)

4. Le territoire de France en Europe est le plus grande parmi les membres de --------------. (ल तेरित्वार द फ्रांस अं यूरोप ए ल प्लु ग्रों पार्मी ले मोंब्र द---------।) (The territory of France in Europe is the largest among the members of -------------.) (यूरोप में फ्रांस का क्षेत्रफल ... . के सदस्यो में सबसे बडा है।)

5. France est dans la deuxième position de -----------. (फ्रांस ए दाँ ला दुज़िएम पोजीशियों द -----------।) (France is in the second position of ---------.) (फ्रांस .... के दूसरे स्थान में है।)

Ans : 1- axis powers 2- Union Européen 3- cinquième république 4- première république de France 5- zone économique exclusif

Exercise 22: Choisissez les bonnes réponses. (शुआज़िस्से ले बोन रेपांस।) (Choose the correct answers.) (सही उत्तरों का चुनाव करें।)

Q 1. What has been an important industry and cultural export of France?

a. Fashion (फैशन) (Mode) (मोद)
b. Sports (खेल) (Sports) (स्पोर)
c. Arms (शस्त्र) (Armes) (आर्म)
d. Music (संगीत) (Musique) (म्यूज़ीक)

Q 2. Since when Fashion been an important industry and cultural export of France?

a. 15th century (15वीं सदी) (Quinzième siècle) (कैन्ज़ीऐम सीऐक्ल)
b. 16th century (16वीं सदी) (Seizième siècle) (सेज़ीएम सीऐक्ल)
c. 17th century (17वीं सदी) (Dix-septième siècle) (दीस-सेतीऐम सीऐक्ल)
d. 20th century (20वीं सदी) (Vingtième siècle) (वैन्तीएम सीऐक्ल)

Q 3. What is fashion called, in French?

a. High fashion (हाई फैशन) (Haute couture) (ओत कूतूर)
b. Sports (खेल) (Sports) (स्पोर)
c. Nourriture (नुरीचूर) (Food) (खाना)
d. Music (संगीत) (Musique) (म्यूज़ीक)

Q 4. Where did fashion originate?

a. Lyon (लियों)
b. Nice (निस)
c. Marseille (मारसेय)
d. Paris (पारी)

Q 5. When did fashion originate?

a. 1860s
b. 1920s
c. 1290s
d. 1970s

Q 6. Which city is one of the world's fashion capitals apart from Paris?

a. Mumbai (मुम्बाई)
b. London (लंदन) (Londres) (लोन्द्र)
c. Tel Aviv (तेल अविव)
d. New Delhi (नई दिल्ली) (न्यू देली)

Q 7. Which city is another one of the world's fashion capitals?

a. Milan (मीलान)
b. Yangon (यान्गोन)
c. Pune (पूने)
d. Kolkata (कोलकाता)

Q 8. Which city is yet another one of the world's fashion capitals?

a. New Delhi (नई दिल्ली) (न्यू देली)
b. Gurugram (गुरुग्राम)
c. Noida (नोएडा)
d. New York City (न्यू यॉर्क सीटी)

Q 9. Who is associated with causing fashion and style to grow in France?

a. Louis XIV (लूई चौदहवां) (लूई कैतोर्ज़)
b. Rahul Gandhi (राहुल गांधी)
c. Louis X (लूई दसवां) (लूई दिस)
d. Narendra Modi (नरेंद्र मोदी)

Q 10. Which is a great French couturier house?

a. Bata (बाटा)
b. Chanel (शानेल)

c. Reebok (रीबोक)
d. Nike (नाईक)

Answers: 1a, 2c, 3a, 4d, 5a, 6b, 7a, 8d, 9a, 10b

Exercise 23: Reliez les mots suivants. (रलिये ले मो सुअिवांता) (Match the following words.) (निम्नलिखित शब्दों का मिलान कीजिए)

French
Q 1. Dior (दिओर)
Q 2. Givenchy (गीवऐन्ची)
Q 3. Grasse (ग्रास)
Q 4. Mont Blanc (मों ब्लां)
Q 5. Dame Blanche (दाम ब्लांश)
Q 6. Grandes Alpes (ग्रां आल्प)
Q 7. Saint-Gervals-les-Bains
Q 8. Chamonix (शामोनी)
Q 9. Italie et France (इताली फ्रांस)
Q 10. Mont Blanc massif (मों ब्लां मासीफ)

English
a. White Lady
b. Couturier house
c. Hiking
d. White Mountain
e. Another couturier house
f. Mountain range
g. Surrounds Mont Blanc
h. First Winter Olympics
i. Mont Blanc Tunnel
j. Perfume industry

Hindi
A. शामोनी
B. दाम ब्लांश
C. ग्रास
D. मों ब्लां
E. गीवऐन्ची
F. ग्रां आल्प
G. सैं जरवाल लेबैं
H. मों ब्लां मासीफ
I. इताली और फ्रांस
J. दिओर

Answers: 1bJ, 2eE, 3jC, 4dD, 5aB, 6fF, 7gG, 8hA, 9iI, 10cH
Note : Above are the names so same written in Hindi column.

Exercise 24: Remplir les espaces vides. (रांपलीर लेज़ैसपास वीदा) (Fill in the blanks.) (रिक्त स्थान भरें।)

The official name of France is la république française (the French republic). Its Population is 68 million people. Its capital is Paris with 11 million people. France's motto is Liberté, Egalité, Fraternité' (Liberty, Equality, Fraternity).

It has a democracy form of government. Its official language is French. Religion-wise, Christians from 65% of the population and Muslims 8%. Its currency is the euro. Its flag is blue, white and red. Its anthem is the "La Marseillaise".

soixante-cinq (सोआसोतं-सैंक) (sixty five) (पैंसठ), population (पोपूलासीयों) (population) (आबादी), Fraternité (फ्रातेरनीते) (Fraternity) (बन्धुत्व), démocratie (देमोक्रासी) (Democracy) (लोकतंत्र), français (फ्रान्से) (French) (फ्रेंच), euro (यूरो), rouge (रूज) (red) (लाल), Marseillaise (मारसेयेज़), république (रेपुबलीक) (republic) (गणतंत्र), Paris (पारी)

1. Le nom officiel de la France est la __________ française. (ल नो ओफिसिएल द ला फ्रांस ए ला _____ फ्रांसेस।)

2. La __________ de la France est 68 million. (ला _____ द ला फ्रांस ए 68 मिलियों।)

3. La capitale de la France est __________. (ला कापितल द ला फ्रांस ए _____ ।)

4. La devise de la France est Liberté, Egalité, __________. (ला दवीज़ द ला फ्रांस ए लीबर्ते, एगालिते, _____ ।)

5. La France est une __________ . (ला फ्रांस ए त्युन _____।)

6. La langue officielle de la France est __________ . (ला लांग ओफिसिएल द ला फ्रांस ए _____ ।)

7. La population chrétienne de France est __________% . (ला पोपुलाशियों क्रेतिएन द फ्रांस ए _____ % .)

8. Sa monnaie est l'__________. (सा मोनाइ ए ल _____।)

9. Son drapeau est bleu, blanc et __________. (सों द्रापो ए ब्ल, ब्लाशं ए _____।)

10. Son hymne est La __________. (सों नीमेन ए ला _____।)

Answers: 1. république (रेपुबलीक) (republic) (गणतंत्र), 2. population (पोपूलासीयों) (population) (आबादी), 3. Paris (पारी), 4. Fraternité (फ्रातेरनीते) (Fraternity) (बन्धुत्व), 5. démocratie (देमोक्रासी) (Democracy) (लोकतंत्र), 6. français (फ्रान्से) (French) (फ्रेंच), 7. soixante-cinq (सोआसोतं-सैंक) (sixty five) (पैंसठ), 8. euro (यूरो), 9. rouge (रूज) (red) (लाल), 10. Marseillaise (मारसेयेज़)

Exercise 25: Remplir les espaces vides. (रांपलीर लेज़ैसपास वीदा) (Fill in the blanks.) (रिक्त स्थान भरें।)

La Seine (ला सेन), Douzième siècle (दूज़ीएम सीऐक्ल) (12वीं सदी), Grec/que (ग्रेक) (ग्रीक), Romain/e (रोमां/रोमेन) (रोमन), Le Palais du Louvre (ल पैले दू लूव्र), Révolution française (रेवोल्यूसीओं फ्रांसेज़), Assemblée nationale (आस्मब्ले नासीओनाल), Le Palais de Versailles (ल पैले द वरसाई), août (अूत), le musée du Louvre (ल म्यूज़े दू लूव्र)

Q 1. The Louvre Museum:__________

Q 2. Seine river: __________

Q 3. Louvre Palace: __________

Q 4. 12th century: __________

Q 5. Palace of Versailles: __________

Q 6. Greek: __________

Q 7. Roman: __________

Q 8. French Revolution: __________

Q 9. National Assembly: __________

Q 10. August: __________

Answers: 1. Le musée du Louvre (ल म्यूज़े दू लूव्र)
2. La Seine (ला सेन)
3. Le Palais du Louvre (ल पैले दू लूव्र)
4. Douzième siècle (दूज़ीएम सीऐक्ल) (12वीं सदी)
5. Le Palais de Versailles (ल पैले द वरसाई)
6. Grec/que (ग्रेक) (ग्रीक)
7. Romain/e (रोमां/रोमेन) (रोमन)
8. Révolution française (रेवोल्यूसीओं फ्रांसेज़)
9. Assemblée nationale (आस्मब्ले नासीओनाल)
10. août (अूत)

Exercise 26: Vrai/Faux (व्रे/फो) (True/False) (सही/गलत)

Le Tour de France est un événement sportif annuel. C'est le plus populaire et le plus suivi. Il se déroule chaque mois de juillet. C'est une vitrine du vélo. C'est aussi une vitrine de la France. En plus, de ses paysages. Il a été créé par Henri Desgrange. Aujourd'hui, la course est organisée par Amaury Sport Organisation (ASO). Le vainqueur gagne 450 000 €. Henri Desgrange, a décidé que le leader porte un maillot jaune. Le Tour commence sur les Champs Élysées.

ल तुर द फ्रॉन्स ए अं एवेनेमो स्पोर्तिफ आनुएल। से ल प्लु पॉपुलेर ए ल प्लू सुइवी। इल स देरुल शाक मुआ द जुइये। सेत इयुन वित्रीन दू वेलो। सेत ओसी इयुन वित्रीन द ला फ्रॉन्स। ऑ प्लु, द से पेईसाज़। इल आ एते क्रिए पार अंरी देग्रांज। ओजूरद्वि, ला कुरस एत ओर्गानिसे पार आमूरी स्पोर ओर्गानिसासियो (आ एस ओ)। ल वांकर गान्य कातर सौ सिन्कोंत मिल एरो। ऑऋ देगरोंज, आ देसीदे क ल लीद्रे पोर्त अं माइओ ज़ोन। ल तुर कोमोन्स सुर ले शों एलिसे।

The Tour de France is an annual sporting event. It is the most popular and the most followed. It takes place every July. It's a bicycle showcase. It is also a showcase of France. In addition, of its landscapes. It was created by Henri Desgrange. Today, the race is organized by Amaury Sport Organization (ASO). The winner wins €450,000. Henri Desgrange, decided that the leader wears a yellow jersey. The Tour begins on the Champs Élysées.

टूर डी फ्रांस एक वार्षिक खेल आयोजन है। यह सबसे लोकप्रिय और सबसे ज्यादा फॉलो किया जाने वाला है। यह हर जुलाई में होता है। यह एक साइकिल शोकेस है। यह फ्रांस का शोकेस भी है। इसके अलावा, इसके परिदृश्य के। इसे हेनरी डेसग्रेंज ने बनाया था। आज, दौड़ का आयोजन अमौरी स्पोर्ट ऑर्गनाइजेशन (एएसओ) द्वारा किया जाता है। विजेता €450,000 जीतता है। हेनरी डेसग्रेंज ने फैसला किया कि नेता पीले रंग की जर्सी पहनता है। टूर चैंप्स एलिसीज़ पर शुरू होता है।

Q1. Le Tour de France n'est pas un événement sportif annuel. (ल तूर द फ्रांस ने पाज़ अं ऐवेनमं स्पोरतीव ऐनुऐला) (The Tour de France is not an annual sports event.) (टूर डी फ्रांस एक वार्षिक खेल आयोजन नहीं है।)

Q2. C'est le plus populaire et le plus suivi. (से ल प्लू पोपुलेर ऐ ल प्लू सूईवी।) (It is the most popular and the most followed.) (यह सबसे लोकप्रिय और सबसे ज्यादा फॉलो किया जाने वाला है।)

Q3. Il se déroule chaque mois de juillet. (इल स देरूल शाक मुआ द ज़ुइये।) (It takes place every July month.) (यह हर जुलाई महीने में होता है।)

Q4. C'est une vitrine du vélo. (सेत्यून वीत्रीन दू वेलो।) (It's a bicycle showcase.) (यह एक साइकिल शोकेस है।)

Q5. C'est aussi une vitrine de la France. (सेत ओसी यून वीत्रीन द ला फ्रांस।) (It is, also, a France showcase.) (यह भी, एक फ्रांस शोकेस है।)

Q6. En plus, de ses paysages. (अं प्लूस, द से पेईसाज़।) (In addition, of its landscapes.) (इसके अलावा, इसके परिदृश्य के।)

Q7. Il a été créé par Henri Desgrange. (ईल आ ऐते क्रेऐ पार अंरी देग्रांजा) (It was created by Henri Desgrange.) (इसेहेनरी डेसग्रेंज ने बनाया था।)

Q8. Le vainqueur gagne 150 000 €. (ल वैंकर गान्य € 150 000.) (The winner wins € 150,000.) (विजेता € 150,000 जीतता है।)

Q9. Le leader porte un maillot vert. (ल लीदर पोत् अं मेईयो वेर।) (The leader wears a green jersey.) (नेता हरे रंग की जर्सी पहनता है।)

Q10. Le Tour ne commence pas sur les Champs Élysées. (ल तूर न कोमो पा सूर ले शांप ऐलीज़े।) (The Tour does not start on the Champs Élysées.) (टूर चैंप्स एलिसीज़ पर शुरू नहीं होता है।)

Answers: 1. Faux (फो) (False) (गलत)
2. Vrai (व्रे) (True) (सही)
3. Vrai (व्रे) (True) (सही)
4. Vrai (व्रे) (True) (सही)
5. Vrai (व्रे) (True) (सही)
6. Vrai (व्रे) (True) (सही)
7. Vrai (व्रे) (True) (सही)

8. Faux (फो) (False) (गलत)
9. Faux (फो) (False) (गलत)
10. Faux (फो) (False) (गलत)

Exercise 27: Chassez l'intrus. (शासे लांत्रू) (Choose the odd one.) (असंगत का चयन करें)

Q 1. a. nord (नो) (north) (उत्तर)
b. Saint-Gervals-les-Bains (सैं-जरवाल-ले-बैं)
c. sud (सूद) (south) (दक्षिण)
d. ouest (वैस्त) (west) (पश्चिम)

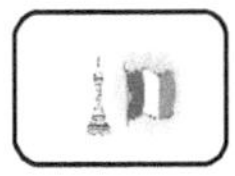

Q 2. a. gauche (गोश) (left) (बायां)
b. droite (द्रोआत) (right) (दांई)
c. à côté de (आ कोते द) (besides) (बगल में)
d. Chamonix (शामोनी)

Q 3. a. tournez (तूरने) (turn) (मुड़े)
b. excusez (एक्सक्यूज़े) (excuse) (क्षमा करें)
c. sortez (सोरते) (exit) (बाहर निकलें)
d. Grandes Alpes (ग्रां आल्प)

Q 4. a. gauche (गोश) (left) (बायां)
b. tout droit (तू द्रोआ) (straight) (सीधा)
c. droite (द्रोआत) (right) (दांई)
d. Italie et France (इताली ऐ फ्रांस)

Q 5. a. montre (मोंत्र) (watch) (घड़ी)
b. horloge (ओरलोज़) (clock) (घड़ी)
c. Mont Blanc massif (मों ब्लां मासीफ)
d. horlogier (आरलोजियेर) (clockmaker) (घड़ीसाज़)

Q 6. a. près de (प्रे द) (near) (निकट)
b. à côté de (आ कोते द) (besides) (बगल में)
c. loin de (लोआं द) (far) (दूर)
d. Dame Blanche (दाम ब्लांश)

Q 7. a. Mont Blanc (मों ब्लां)
b. avion (आविओं) (aeroplane) (विमान)
c. bus (ब्युस) (bus) (बस)
d. taxi (ताक्सी) (taxi) (टैक्सी)

Q 8. a. Grasse (ग्रास)
b. droite (द्रोआत) (right) (दांई)
c. sud (सूद) (south) (दक्षिण)

d. gauche (गोश) (left) (बायां)

Q 9. a. Givenchy (गीवऐन्ची)
b. souris (सूरी) (mouse) (चूहा)
c. rat (रा) (rat) (चूहा)
d. tigre (तीग्र) (tiger) (बाघ)

Q 10.a. lion (लीओं) (lion) (सिंह)
b. Dior (दिओर)
c. souris (सूरी) (mouse) (चूहा)
d. chien (शीआं) (dog) (कुत्ता)

Answer: 1b, 2d, 3d, 4d, 5c, 6d, 7a, 8a, 9a, 10b

Exercise 28: Pourquoi avez-vous choisis la France? (पूरकुआ आवे वू शोआसी ला फ्रांस?) **(Why did you choose France?)** (आपने फ्रांस को क्यों चुना?)

Answer:
J'ai choisi la France parce que mon pays l'Inde est le pays en voie de développement, tandis que la France est le pays déjà développé. Alors la qualité de vie est beaucoup meilleure que celle de l'Inde. Dans 1997, on a mené une enquête auprès de résidents de vingt pays. La majorité des répondants ont classé la France dans la liste des dix pays où ils aimeraient le plus vivre. La plupart considerèrent la France comme une nation généreuse, paisible et humaine, et trouvent les français honnêtes, aimables et polis.

जे सोआसी ला फ्रॉन्स पार्स क मो पेई लांद ए ल पेई ओं वुआ द देवेलपमो, तोंदी क ला फ्रॉन्स ए ल पेई देजा देवेलोपे। अलोर ला कालिते द वि ए बोकू मइयर क सेल द लांद। दॉ 1997, ओ आ मैने युन ओंकेत ओपेर द रेज़ीदों द वन्य पेई। ला माजोरीते दे रेपोंदों ओं क्लासे ला फ्रॉन्स दॉ ला लिस्त दे दीज़ पेई उ इल्ज़ एमेरों ल प्लूस विव्र। ला पलुपार कोनसीदेरों ला फ्रॉन्स कॉम युन नेसों जेनेर्ज़, पज़िबल ए उमेन, ए त्रुवों ले फ्रॉन्सेज़ ओनेत, एमाब्ल ए पोली।

I have chosen France because my country i.e. India is a developing country whereas France is already a developed country. The quality of life is much better as compared to India. A 1997 survey of people in 20 countries found that the majority placed France in the top ten list of countries where they would like to live. Most consider France a generous, peaceful & compassionate nation & they see French as honest, friendly and polite.

मैंने फ्रांस को इसलिए चुना है क्योंकि मेरा देश यानी भारत एक विकासशील देश है जबकि फ्रांस पहले से ही एक विकसित देश है। भारत की तुलना में जीवन की गुणवत्ता काफी बेहतर है। 1997 में 20 देशों के लोगों के एक सर्वेक्षण में पाया गया कि अधिकांश लोगों ने फ्रांस को उन देशों की शीर्ष दस सूची में रखा जहां वे रहना चाहते हैं। अधिकांश लोग फ्रांस को एक उदार, शांतिपूर्ण और दयालु राष्ट्र मानते हैं और वे फ्रेंच लोगों को ईमानदार, मैत्रीपूर्ण और विनम्र मानते हैं।

Exercise 29: Choisissez les bonnes réponses. (शुआज़िस्से ले बोन रेपांस।) **(Choose the correct answers.)** (सही उत्तरों का चुनाव करें।)

Q 1. Quel est le mot latin de France? (केल ऐ ल मो लातां द फ्रांस?) (What is the Latin word for France?) (फ्रांस का पहले क्या नाम था?)
a. Francia (फ्रान्सीया) (Francia) (फ्रान्सीया)
b. fashion (फैशन) (mode) (मोद)

c. sports (खेल) (sports) (स्पोर)
d. animal (जानवर) (animal) (आनीमाल)

Q 2. La France est un pays développé avec______économie. (ला फ्रांस ऐतून पेय देवेलोप्पे आवेक____
(France is a developed country with______economy.) (फ्रांस एक विकसित देश है ______आर्थिक स्थिति
a. le troisième plus grand. (ल त्रोआज़ीएम प्लू ग्रां।) (the third largest.) (तीसरी बड़ी।)
b. le deuxième plus grand. (ल दसीएम प्लू ग्रां।) (the second largest.) (दूसरी बड़ी।)
c. le sixième plus grand. (ल सिसीएम प्लू ग्रां।) (the sixth largest.) (छठी बड़ी।)
d. le plus grand. (ल त्प्लू ग्रां।) (the largest.) (पहली बड़ी।)

Q 3. OTAN signifie_____. (ओतां सीगनीफि______।) (NATO stands for_____.) (नाटो का पूरा नाम______।)
a. Organisation du Traité de l'Atlantique Nord. (ओरगानीज़ासीओं दू त्रेते द लातलांतीक नोर।) (North Atlantic Treaty Organization.) (उत्तर अटलांटिक ट्रीटी संगठन।)
b. Nobel Américain Trio Organization. (नोबेल अमेरीकां ट्रायो ओरगानीज़ासीओं।) (Nobel American Trio Organization.) (नोबल अमेरिकन ट्रायो ओरगनआईज़ेशन।)
c. Nouveaux Atlanta Trailé Octobre. (नुवो अटलांटा ट्रायले ओकतोब्र।) (New Atlanta Trail October.) (नया अटलांटा ट्रायल अक्टूबर।)
d.Nouvelle Américain Trailé Organization. (नुवेल अमेरीकां ट्रायले ओरगानीज़ासीओं।) (New American Treaty Organization.) (न्यु अमेरिकन ट्रीटी संगठन।)

Q 4. Quel est la signification de mot "francophonie"? (केल ऐ ला सिग्निफिकाशियों द मो "फ्रांकोफोनी"?) (What is the meaning of the word "francophonie"?) ("फ्रांकोफोनी" का क्या मतलब होता है?)
a. Les pays où on parle français. (ले पेय अू ओं पार्ल फ्रान्से।) (The countries where we speak French.) (जिन देशों में हम फ्रेंच बोलते हैं।)
b. musique (म्यूज़ीक) music (संगीत)
c. sports (स्पोर) sports (खेल)
d. vu (वू) seen (देखा)

Q 5. Combien de touristes visitent la France en l'annee? (कोंबियां द टूरीस्त विसित ला फ्रांस अं लाने?) (How many tourists visit France in a year?) (साल में कितने टूरिस्ट फ्रांस घूमने आते हैं?)
a. quatre-vingt-treize million (केत्र-वैं-त्रेज़ मीलीयों) (ninety three million) (तिरानवे मिलियन)
b. quarante-huit million (कैरांत-वुईत मीलीयों) (forty eight million) (अड़तालीस मिलियन)
c. soixante-seize million (स्वासोंत-सेज़ मीलीयों) (seventy six million) (छिहत्तर मिलियन)
d. quatre-vingt-trois million (केत्र-वैं-त्रोआ मीलीयों) (eighty three million) (तिरासी मिलियन)

Answers: 1a, 2c, 3a, 4a, 5d

Exercise 30: Reliez les mots suivants. (रलिये ले मो सुअिवांता) (Match the following words.) (निम्नलिखित शब्दों का मिलान की जिए।)

French
1. EDF (अदेऐफ)
2. ELE Aquitaine (ऐले आकीतेन)
3. Alcatel (आल्काटेल)

4. Générale des eaux (जेनेराल देज़ ओ)
5. Lecerc (लसेर्क)

English

a) Hypermarket
b) Electricity
c) Petrol
d) Electronic
e) Mineral water

Hindi

A. (ईडीऐफ)
B. (ऐले आकीतेन)
C. (जेनेराल देज़ ओ)
D. (आल्काटेल)
E. (लसेर्क)

Answers: 1bA, 2cB, 3dD, 4eC, 5aE

Exercise 31: Lisez et répondez. (लिसे ऐ रेपोंदे) (Read and give the answer) (पढ़िए और जवाब दीजिए)

France possesses a wide variety of landscapes, from coastal plains in the north and west to mountain ranges of the Alps in the southeast, the Massif Central in the south central and Pyrenees in the southwest. Due to its numerous overseas departments and territories scattered across the planet, France possesses the second-largest Exclusive Economic Zone (EEZ) in the world, covering 11,035,000 km^2 (4,260,000 mi^2), just behind the EEZ of the United States (11,351,000 km^2 / 4,383,000 mi^2), but ahead of the EEZ of Australia (8,148,250 km^2 / 4,111,312 mi^2). Its EEZ covers approximately 8% of the total surface of all the EEZs of the world.

At 4,810.45 metres (15,782 ft) above sea level, the highest point in Western Europe, Mont Blanc, is situated in the Alps on the French and Italian border. France also has extensive river systems such as the Seine, the Loire, the Garonne, and the Rhone, which divides the Massif Central from the Alps and flows into the Mediterranean Sea at the Camargue.

The constitution of the Fifth Republic was approved by referendum on 28th September 1958. It greatly strengthened the authority of the executive in relation to parliament. The executive branch itself has two leaders: the President of the Republic, who is head of state and is elected directly by universal adult suffrage for a 5-year term (formerly 7 years), and the Government, led by the president-appointed Prime Minister. The French parliament is a bicameral legislature comprising a National Assembly and a Senate.

Q 1. Quel sont les noms des rivières en France ? (केल सों ले नों दे रीवीऐर अं फ्रांस ?) (What are the names of rivers in France?) (फ्रांस में नदियों के नाम क्या हैं?)

Q 2. Qui a approuvé la constitution de la cinquième république et quand ? (की आ अप्रूवे ला कांस्टीतूसीयों द ला सैंकीऐम रेपूब्लिक ए कां ?) (Who approved the constitution of the fifth republic and when?) (पांचवें गणतंत्र के संविधान को किसने और कब मंजूरी दी?)

Q 3. Quelle est la signification de EEZ ? (केल ऐ ला सीगनीफीकासीयों द EEZ ?) (What is the full form of EEZ?) (ईईजे का क्या मतलब है?)

Q 4. Où est le mont blanc situé ? (ऊ ए ल मों ब्लां सीचुऐ ?) (Where is Mont Blanc situated?) (मोंट ब्लांक कहाँ स्थित है?)

Q 5. Le parlement français est-il une législature bicamérale ? (ल पारलमं फ्रांसे ऐतील अून लेजीसलाचूर बीकामेराल ?) Is the French parliament a bicameral legislature? (क्या फ्रांस की संसद द्विसदनीय विधायिका है?)

Answers: 1. Seine, Loire, Garonne and Rhône
2. Referendum On 28th September
3. Exclusive Economic Zone
4. In the Alps border of France and Italy
5. Yes

Exercise 32: Remplir les espaces vides. (रांपलीर लेज़्रैसपास वीदा) (Fill in the blanks.) (रिक्त स्थान भरें।)

occupation (ओकूपासीओं) (पेशा), économique (ऐकोनोमीक) (आर्थिक), connexions (कोनेकसीओं) (सम्बन्ध), victorieux (वीकतोरीअ) (विजयी), libération (लीबेरासीओं) **(मुक्ति)**

Q1. victorious: __________

Q2. occupation: __________

Q3. liberation: __________

Q4. economic: __________

Q5. connections: __________

Answers: 1. victorieux (वीकतोरीअ) (विजयी), 2. occupation (ओकूपासीओं) (पेशा), 3. libération (लीबेरासीओं) (मुक्ति), 4. économique (ऐकोनोमीक) (आर्थिक), 5. connexions (कोनेकसीओं) (सम्बन्ध)

Exercise 33: Vrai/Faux (व्रे/फो) (True/False) (सही/गलत)

1. La France est l'un des principaux membres de l'union europeenne. (ला फ्रांस ए लं दे प्रिंसिपो मोंब्र द लायूनियों योरोपेयां।) (France is a leading member State of the European Union.) (फ्रांस यूरोपीय संघ का एक प्रमुख सदस्य राज्य है।)

2. Le Mont blanc est à la frontière entre l'Espagne et la France. (ल मों ब्लां ऐ आ ला फ्रोन्तीयर अंत्र लेस्पान्य ऐ ला फ्रांस ।) (Mont Blanc is on the Spain and France border.) (मों ब्लां स्पेन और फ्रांस की सीमा पर है।)

3. Le président de la république en France est élu par suffrage universel adulte.(ल प्रेसिदां द ला रेपुब्लिक अं फ्रांस ऐ ऐलू पार सुफ्राज़ यूनिवेर्सेल अदुल्त।) (The president of the Republic of France is elected by universal adult suffrage.) (फ्रांस गणराज्य के राष्ट्रपति का चुनाव सार्वभौमिक वयस्क मताधिकार द्वारा किया जाता है।)

4. En France, les juges font la loi. (अं फ्रांस, ले जूज फों ला लोआ।) (In France, judges make the law.) (फ्रांस में, न्यायाधीश कानून बनाते हैं।)

5. La France est le centre mondial de l'art, philosophie et la science.(ला फ्रांस ऐ ल संट्र मोंदीयाल द लार्, फिलोसोफी ऐ ला सियांस।) (France is a global centre of philosophy, art and science.) (फ्रांस दर्शन, कला और विज्ञान का वैश्विक केंद्र है।)

Answers: 1. Vrai (व्रे) (True) (सही), 2. Faux (फो) (False) (गलत), 3. Vrai (व्रे) (True) (सही), 4. Faux (फो) (False) (गलत), 5. Vrai (व्रे) (True) (सही)

Exercise 34: Chassez l'intrus. (शासे लांत्रू।) **(Choose the odd one.)** (असंगत का चयन करें।)

Q 1. a. gauche (गोश) (left) (बायां)
b. droite (द्रोआत) (right) (दांई)
c. à côté de (आ कोते द) (besides) (बगल में)
d. parlement (पारलमो) (parliament) (संसद)

Q 2. a. légal (लेगाल) (legal) (कानूनी)
b. avion (आविओं) (aeroplane) (विमान)
c. bus (ब्युस) (bus) (बस)
d. taxi (ताक्सी) (taxi) (टैक्सी)

Q 3. a. droit (द्रोआ) (law) (कानून)
b. droite (द्रोआत) (right) (दांई)
c. sud (सूद) (south) (दक्षिण)
d. gauche (गोश) (left) (बायां)

Q 4. a. civil (सिविल) (civil) (सिविल)
b. souris (सूरी) (mouse) (चूहा)
c. rat (रा) (rat) (चूहा)
d. tigre (तीग्र) (tiger) (बाघ)

Q 5.a. lion (लीओं) (lion) (सिंह)
b. services (सेरवीस) (services) (सेवा)
c. souris (सूरी) (mouse) (चूहा)
d. chien (शीआं) (dog) (कुत्ता)

Answer: 1d, 2a, 3a, 4a, 5b

Exercise 35: Dites vrai ou faux. (दीत व्रे उ फो।) **(Tell true or false.)** (सही या गलत बताओ।)

1. Le français est aussi connu comme langue du commerce. (ल फ्रांसे एतोस्सी कोन्यु कॉम लांग द्यु कॉमर्स।) (French is also known as language of commerce.) (फ्रेंच को वाणिज्य की भाषा के रूप में भी जाना जाता है।)

2. Les écoles publiques françaises dispensent un enseignement gratuit et laïc. (ले ज़ेकोल प्यूबलीक फ्रांसेस दिसपांस अं ओंसीन्यमों ग्रातुइ ए लाइक।) (French government schools give free and secular education.) (फ्रांसीसी सरकारी स्कूल मुफ्त और धर्मनिरपेक्ष शिक्षा देते हैं।)

3. L'islam est la sixième religion en France. (लिसलाम ए ला सीज़िएम रिलिज़ियों अं फ्रांस।) (Islam is the sixth religion in France.) (फ्रांस में इस्लाम छठा धर्म है।)

4. La tour Eiffel a été faite en 1889. (ला तूर इफेल अ एते फेत अं 1889.) (Eiffel tower was made in 1889.) (एफिल टावर का निर्माण 1889 में हुआ था।)

5. La hauteur de la tour est de 325 mètres. (लोतर द ला तूर ए द 325 मेत्र।) (The height of the tower is 325 meters.) (टावर की ऊंचाई 325 मीटर है।)

6. L'Arc de Triomphe rend hommage à ceux qui ont combattu et sont morts pour la France pendant la Révolution française et les guerres napoléoniennes. (लार्क द त्रवांप रोंद ओमाज़ अ स कीओं कोंबात्यु ए सों मोर्त पूर ला फ्रांस पोंदों ला रेवोल्यूशियों फ्रांसेस ए ल गर नेपोलियन्।) (The Arc de Triomphe was built to honor those who fought and died for France in the French Revolutionary and the Napoleonic Wars.) (आर्क डी ट्रायम्फ उन लोगों के सम्मान में बनाया गया था जो फ्रांसीसी क्रांतिकारी और नेपोलियन युद्धों में फ्रांस के लिए लड़े और मारे गए।)

7. Le yen est la monnaie de la france. (ल येन ए ला मोनेई द ला फ्रांस।) (Yen is the currency of France.) (येन फ्रांस की मुद्रा है।)

8. Paris est reconnue pour sa couture de haute couture et ses boutiques haut de gamme. (पारी ए रकोन्यु पूर सा ओत् कोंत्यूर ए से बूतीक् ओत् द गाम्।) (Paris is known for its haute couture couture and high-end boutiques.) (पेरिस अपने हाउते कॉउचर और उच्च-स्तरीय बुटीक के लिए जाना जाता है।)

9. 75% de la population française vit dans les zones urbaines. (75% द ला पोपुलाशियों फ्रांसेस वीत दाँ ले जोन् अरबेन।) (75% of the French population lives in urban areas.) (75% फ्रांसीसी आबादी शहरी क्षेत्रों में रहती है।)

10. Le drapeau français est tricolore (bleu, blanc et rouge). (ल द्रापो फ्रांसे ए त्रीकूलर (ब्ल, ब्लाश ए रूज़।) (The French flag is tricolor (blue, white and red)). (फ्रांसीसी ध्वज तिरंगा नीला, सफेद और लाल है।)

Réponse (रेपोंस) (Answer) (उत्तर): 1-vrai (right) (सही) 2-vrai (right) (सही) 3-faux (wrong) (गलत) 4-vrai (right) (सही) 5- faux (wrong) (गलत) 6-vrai (right) (सही) 7-faux (wrong) (गलत) 8-vrai (right) (सही) 9-vrai (right) (सही) 10-vrai (right) (सही)

Exercise 36: Répondez aux questions suivantes. (रपोंदे ओ केसचियों सुइवो।) (Answer the following questions.) (निम्नलिखित सवालों का जवाब दें।)

1. Quelle est le capital de France ? (केले ल कापीताल द फ्रांस ?) (What is the capital of France?) (फ्रांस की राजधानी क्या है?)

2. De quelle couleur est le drapeau de France ? (द केल कूलर ए ल द्रापो द फ्रांस ?) (What's the colour of French flag?) (फ्रांस का झंडा किस रंग का है?)

3. Quel est le pain traditionnel de France ? (केले ल पां त्रादिशियोंनल द फ्रांस ?) (What is the traditional bread of France?) (फ्रांस की पारंपरिक रोटी क्या है?)

4. Pourquoi on appelle la France L'Hexagone ? (पूरक्वा ओं नापेल ला फ्रांस लेग्जागोन ?) (Why is France called L'Hexagone?) (फ्रांस को हेक्सागोन क्यों कहा जाता है?)

5. Nommez quelques fleuves français. (नोमे केल्क फ्लव फ्रांसे।) (Name some French rivers.) (कुछ फ्रांसीसी नदियों के नाम बताइए।)

6. Quelle rivière traverse Paris ? (केल रिवेर त्रावर्स पारी ?) (Which river crosses Paris?) (कौन सी नदी पेरिस को पार करती है?)

7. De quels pays La France, est-elle entourée ? (द केल पेइ ला फ्रांस, एतेल अंतूरे ?) (France is surrounded by which countries?) (फ्रांस किन देशों से घिरा है?)

8. Nommez quelques pays ou les gens parlent français. (नोमे केल्क पेइ उ ले जन पार्लां फ्रांसे।) (Name some countries where people speak French.) (कुछ ऐसे देशों के नाम बताइए जहां लोग फ्रेंच बोलते हैं।)

9. Nommez quelques sports célèbres de France. (नोमे केल्क स्पोर्त सेलेब्र द फ्रांस।) (Name some famous sports in France.) (फ्रांस के कुछ प्रसिद्ध खेलों के नाम लिखिए।)

10. Quel est la devise de la république ? (केले ला दवीस द ला रेप्यूबलीक ?) (What is the motto of the republic?) (फ्रांसीसी गणराज्य का आदर्श वाक्य क्या है?)

Réponse (रेपोंस) (Answer) (उत्तर):

1- La capitale de la France est Paris. (ला कापिताल द ला फ्रांस ए पारी।) (The capital of France is Paris.) (फ्रांस की राजधानी पेरिस है।)

2- Le drapeau francais est bleu, blanc et rouge. (ल द्रापो फ्रांसे ए ब्ल, ब्लांक ए रूज़।) (The French flag is blue, white and red.) (फ्रांसीसी झंडा नीला, सफेद और लाल है।)

3- La baguette est le pain traditionnel de France. (ला बगेत ए ल पां त्रादिशियों द फ्रांस।) (The baguette is the traditional bread of France.) (बगेत फ्रांस की पारंपरिक रोटी है।)

4- On appelle la France l'Hexagone parce que la carte de la France a plus ou moins la forme d'un hexagone.(ओनापेल ला फ्रांस लेग्जागोन पार्सक् ला कार्त द ला फ्रांस अ प्लु उ मुआ ला फोर्म द नेग्जागोन।) (France is called the Hexagon because the map of France has more or less the shape of a hexagon.) (फ्रांस को षट्भुज कहा जाता है क्योंकि फ्रांस के नक्शे में कमोबेश एक षट्भुज के आकार का है।)

5- La Seine, le Rhône, la Garonne, la Loire sont les fleuves français. (ला सेन, ल रोन, ला गारोन, ला लुआ सों ले फ्लव फ्रांसे।) (The Seine, the Rhône, the Garonne, the Loire are the French rivers.) (सीन, रोन, गैरोन, लॉयर फ्रांसीसी नदियां हैं।)

6- La Seine traverse Paris. (ला सेन त्रावर्स पारी।) (The Seine crosses Paris.) (सीन पेरिस को पार करती है।)

7- La France est entourée par le Belgique, l'Angleterre, le Luxembourg, l'Italie, la Suisse et l'Espagne. (ला फ्रांस ए ओंतूर्ने पार ल बेल्जिक, लांजलेतेर, ल लूग्जेमबर्ग, लीताली, ला सुइस ए लेस्पान्या) (France is surrounded by Belgium, England, Luxembourg, Italy, Switzerland and Spain.) (फ्रांस बेल्जियम, इंग्लैंड, लक्जमबर्ग, इटली, स्विटजरलैंड और स्पेन से घिरा है।)

8- Le Mexique, le Belgique, la Suisse sont les pays où les gens parlent français. (ल मेक्जीक, ल बेल्जीक, ला सुइस सों ले पेइ ऊ ले जों पार्ल फ्रांसे।) (Mexico, Belgium, Switzerland are the countries where people speak French.) (मेक्सिको, बेल्जियम, स्विटजरलैंड ऐसे देश हैं जहां लोग फ्रेंच बोलते हैं।)

9- Les sports les plus populaires sont le football, le rugby, le cyclisme et le tennis. (ले स्पोर्त ले प्लु पोपुलेर सों ल फुतबॉल, ल रग्बी, ल साइक्लिज्म ए ल तेनिस।) (The most popular sports are Football, Rugby, Cycling and Tennis.) (फुटबॉल, रग्बी, साइकिलिंग और टेनिस सबसे लोकप्रिय खेल हैं।)

10- Liberté, égalité, fraternité est la devise de la République française. (लीबर्ते, एगालिते, फ्रातरनिते ए ला दवीस द ला रेप्यूबलीक फ्रांसे।) (Liberty, equality, fraternity is the motto of the French Republic.) (स्वतंत्रता, समानता, बंधुत्व फ्रांसीसी गणराज्य का आदर्श वाक्य है।)

Exercise 37: Nommez. (नोमे।) (Tell name.) (नाम बताओ।)

1. Deux monument français. (द मोन्यूमों फ्रांसे।) (Two French monuments.) (दो फ्रांसीसी स्मारक।)

2. Deux vins français. (द वाँ फ्रांसे।) (Two French wines.) (दो फ्रेंच वाइन।)

3. Deux fromages français. (द फ्रॉमाज़ फ्रांसे।) (Two French cheeses.) (दो फ्रेंच चीज।)

4. Deux voitures françaises. (द वोत्यूर फ्रांसेस।) (Two French cars.) (दो फ्रेंच कारें।)

5. Deux parfums français. (द पारफ्युम फ्रांसे।) (Two French perfumes.) (दो फ्रेंच परफ्यूम।)

6. Deux pains français. (द पाँ फ्रांसे।) (Two French breads.) (दो फ्रेंच ब्रेड।)

7. Deux musées français. (द म्यूज़े फ्रांसे।) (Two French museums.) (दो फ्रांसीसी संग्रहालय।)

8. Deux villes françaises. (द वील फ्रांसेस।) (Two French cities) (दो फ्रांसीसी शहर।)

9. Deux chaines françaises. (द शेन फ्रासेस।) (Two French channels.) (दो फ्रेंच चैनल।)

10. Deux journaux français. (द जूर्नों फ्रासे।) (Two French newspapers.) (दो फ्रांसीसी समाचार पत्र।)

Réponse (रेपोंस) (Answer) (उत्तर):
1- la tour Eiffel et le Louvre (ल तूर इफेल ए ल लूव्र) (the Eiffel Tower and the Louvre) (एफिल टॉवर और लौवर)

2- le bordeaux et le bourgogne (ल बोर्दो ए ल बूरगोन्य) (Bordeaux and Burgundy) (बोर्डो और बरगंडी)

3- le camembert et le roquefort (ल कमेमबर्त ए ल रोक्फोर्त) (Camembert and Roquefort) (कैमेम्बर्ट और रोक्फोर्ट)

4- le Peugeot et le Renault (ल पगोत् ए ल रनोल्त) (Peugeot et Renault) (प्यूज़ो और रेनॉल्ट)

5- le Calvin Klein et le chanel (ल कलविन क्लेन ए ल शनेल) (Calvin Klein and chanel) (केल्विन क्लेन और चैनल)

6- la baguette le Pain aux Noix (ला बगत ल पां ओ नुआ) (baguette and walnut bread) (बैगूएट और अखरोट की रोटी)

7- le musée de Louvre et le musée d'Orsay (ल म्यूज़े द लूव्र ए ल म्यूज़े दोर्से) (The Louvre Museum and the Orsay Museum) (लौवर संग्रहालय और ओरसे संग्रहालय)

8- le paris et la nice (ल पारी ए ला नीस) (Paris and Nice) (पेरिस और नीस)

9- la france 2 et la canal + (ला फ्रांस 2 ए ला कनाल +) (France 2 and canal +) (फ़्रांस 2 और कनाल +)

10- le monde et le figaro (ल मोंद ए ल फिगारो) (monde and figro) (मोंडे और फिग्रो)

Exercise 38: Reliez les mots avec l'image. (रलिये ल मो आवे लीमाज्रा) (Link the words to the image.) (शब्दों को छवि से लिंक करें।)

1. Louvre

a. 

2. Le Sacré-Cœur

b. 

3. Notre Dame

c. 

4. L'Arc de Triomphe

d. 

5. Le centre George Pompidou

e. 

Réponse (रेपोंस) (Answer) (उत्तर): 1-d, 2-a, 3-e, 4-c, 5-b

Exercise 39: Et dans votre pays ? (ऐ दां वोत्र पेई ?) (And in your country?) (और आपके देश में?)

1. Les monuments (ले मोन्यमो) (The monuments) (स्मारकों)

2. Les fleuves (ले फ्लव) (Rivers) (नदियां)

3. Les pays voisins (ले पेइ व्आजां) (Neighboring countries) (पड़ोसी देश)

4. Les symbols (ले सिंबल) (Symbols) (प्रतीक)

5. L'hymne national (लीमेन नाश्योनाल) (The national anthem) (राष्ट्रगान)

Réponse (रेपोंस) (Answer) (उत्तर):
1- Taj Mahal (Taj Mahal) (ताजमहल)

2- Le Ganges (Ganga) (गंगा)

3- Le Pakistan, la Chine, le Bangladesh (Pakistan, China, Bangladesh) (पाकिस्तान, चीन, बांग्लादेश)

4- Le Chakra d'Ashoka (Ashoka Chakra) (अशोक चक्र)

5- Jan Gan Man (Jan Gan Man) (जन गण मन)

Exercise 40: Associez les villes suivantes à ce pour quoi elles sont connues. (आसोसीऐ ले विल सुईवांत आ स पूर कैल सों कोनु ।) (Associate the following cities with what they are known for.) (निम्नलिखित शहरों को उनके साथ संबद्ध करें जिनके लिए वे जाने जाते हैं।)

1. Lyon

2. Toulouse

3. Cannes
4. Strasbourg

5. Marseille

a. le festival du film (film festival) (फिल्म समारोह)

b. L'industrie de soie (silk industry) (रेशम उद्योग)

c. l'industrie aéronautiques (aeronautical industry) (वैमानिक उद्योग)

d. le siège du parlement européen (european parliament) (यूरोपियन संसद)

e. le port (port) (पोर्ट)

Réponse (रेपोंस) (Answer) (उत्तर): 1-b, 2-c, 3-a, 4-d, 5-e

Exercise 41: Complétez les phrases suivantes. (कोम्प्लेते ले फ्रास सुईवांत।) (Complete the following sentences.) (निम्नलिखित वाक्यों को पूरा करो।)

La tour Eiffel est construite en ___________ (1) par___________ (2). (1. The Eiffel Tower was built in ___________ (1) by ___________ (2).) (एफिल टॉवर ___________ (1) में ___________ (2) द्वारा बनाया गया था।)
La tour Eiffel mesure ___________ (3). (The Eiffel Tower measures ___________ (3).) (एफिल टावर की माप ___________ (3) है।)

Notre Dame est un _______ (4) située en plein cœur de _______ (5). (Notre Dame is a _______ (4) located in the heart of _______ (5).) (नोट्रे डेम एक _______ (4) है जो _______ (5) के केंद्र में स्थित है।)
Le Sacré-cœur est situé sur la colline________(6) (The Sacred Heart is located on the hill ________(6)) (सेक्रेड हार्ट पहाड़ी पर स्थित है ________(6))

L'Arc de triomphe est construite par ________ (7) pour _________(8). (The Arc de Triomphe was built by ________ (7) for _________ (8).) (L'Arc de triomphe को ________ (7) द्वारा _________ (8) के लिए बनाया गया था।)

Le Louvre est plus grand __________ (9) ou on trouve les œuvres connues comme ___________ (10) et ___________ (11). (The Louvre is big __________ (9) where we find the works known as ___________ (10) and ___________ (11). (Louvre बड़ा __________ (9) है जहां हम ___________ (10) और ___________ (11) के रूप में जाने जाने वाले कार्यों को पाते हैं।)

Réponse (रेपोंस) (Answer) (उत्तर):

1- 1889

2- Gustave Eiffel (गुस्ताव एफिल)

3- 325 mètres (325 metres) (325 मीटर)

4- monument (monument) (स्मारकों)

5- l'ile de la Cité (Island of the City) (शहर का द्वीप)

6- Montmartre

7- Napoléon (Napoleon) (नेपोलियन)

8- temoigner des victoires des armées françaises (bear witness of victories of the French armies) (फ्रांसीसी सेनाओं की जीत के साक्षी बनें)

9- musée (museum) (संग्रहालय)

10- la Jaconde de Leonard de Vinci (Mona Lisa by Leonardo da Vinci) (लियोनार्डो द विंची द्वारा मोना लिसा)

11- la Venus de Milo (the Venus of Milo)

Exercise 42: Corrigez les fautes. (कोरीज़े ले फोता) (Correct the mistakes.) (गलतियों को सुधारें।)

1. Le beaujolais est un fleuve français. (ल बोजूलेजे अं फ्लव फ्रासें।) (The Beaujolais is a French river.) (ब्यूजोलिस एक फ्रांसीसी नदी है।)

2. Lyon est connue pour son industrie aéronautique. (लेयो ए कोन्यु पूर सों ओनदस्त्री एरोनातीक्।) (Lyon is known for its aeronautical industry.) (ल्यों अपने वैमानिकी उद्योग के लिए जाना जाता है।)

3. Toulouse est connue pour le festival du film. (तूलूस ए कोन्यु पूर ल फेस्तिवाल द्यु फिल्म ।) (Toulouse is known for the film festival.) (टूलूज़ फिल्म समारोह के लिए जाना जाता है।)

4. Cannes est connue pour son port. (केन् से कोन्नयु पूर सों पोर्त।) (Cannes is known for its port.) (कान्स अपने पोर्ट के लिए प्रसिद्ध है।)

5. Le reblochon est un vin français. (ल रब्लकों ए अं वाँ फ्रासेंस।) (Reblochon is a French wine.) (रेब्लोचॉन एक फ्रेंच वाइन है।)

Réponse (रेपोंस) (Answer) (उत्तर):
1- Le beaujolais est un vin français. (ल बोजूलेजे अं वाँ फ्रासें।) (Beaujolais is a French wine.) (ब्यूजोलिस एक फ्रेंच वाइन है।)

2-Toulouse est connue pour son industrie aéronautique. (तूलूस ए कोन्यु पूर सों ओनदस्त्री एरोनातीक्।) (Toulouse is known for its aeronautical industry.) (टूलूज़ अपने वैमानिकी उद्योग के लिए जाना जाता है।)

3- Cannes est connue pour le festival du film. (केन् से कोन्नयु पूर ल फेस्तिवाल द्यु फिल्म।) (Cannes is known for the film festival.) (कान्स फिल्म फेस्टिवल के लिए जाना जाता है।)

4- Marseille est connue pour son port. (मार्सेइ ए कोन्यू पूर सों पोर्त।) (Marseille is known for its port.) (मार्सिले अपने पोर्ट के लिए जाना जाता है।)

5- Le reblochon est un fromage français. (ल रब्लकों ए अं फ्रॉमाज़ फ्रासेंस।) (Reblochon is a French cheese.) (रेब्लोचोन एक फ्रेंच चीज है।)

Exercise 43: Choisissez la bonne réponse. (शुआज़िस्से ले बोन रेपांस।) (Choose the correct answer.) (सही उत्तर का चयन करें।)

1. 'Prise de la Bastille' s'est produit ? ('परीज़ द ला बास्ति' से प्रोदुई ?) ('Storming of the Bastille' occured on?) ('स्टॉर्मिंग ऑफ द बैस्टिल' कब हुआ था?)

14 juillet (जुलिए) (July) (जुलाई), 1789
14 juillet (जुलिए) (July) (जुलाई), 1798
14 juillet (जुलिए) (July) (जुलाई), 1777
14 juillet (जुलिए) (July) (जुलाई), 1796

2. La société française était divisée en ? (ल सोसियतें फ्रांसे एते दिविज़े ऑ ?) (French society was divided into?) (फ्रांसीसी समाज में विभाजित किया गया था?)

Deux Domaines (द दोमैन) (Two estates) (दो सम्पदा)
Quatre Domaines (कात्र दोमैन) (Four estates) (चार सम्पदा)
Trois Domaines (त्रुआ दोमैन) (Three estates) (तीन सम्पदा)
Aucun de ceux-ci (ओकां द सअ-सी) (None of these) (इनमें से कोई नहीं)

3. Qui a écrit le livre « Social Contract » ? (की आ एकृत ल लिव्र « सोशल कॉन्ट्रैक्ट » ?) (Who wrote the book 'Social Contract'?) ('सोशल कॉन्ट्रैक्ट' पुस्तक किसने लिखी है?)

Abbe Sleyes (अब्बे स्लीयस)
Montesqueu (मोंटेस्क्ल्यू)
Rousseau (रूसो)
Aucun de ceux-ci (ओकां द सअ-सी)

4. Lequel des suivants constituait la classe privilégiée ? (लकेल दे सुइवो कोंस्तितूए ला क्लास प्रीविलाज़े ?) (Which of the following constituted the privileged class?) (निम्नलिखित में से किसने विशेषाधिकार प्राप्त वर्ग का गठन किया?)
Clergé et paysans (क्लेरज़े ए पेइज़ओ) (Clergy and peasants) (पादरी और किसान)
Paysans et noblesse (पेइज़ओ ए नॉबलेस) (Peasants and nobility) (किसान और बड़प्पन)
Aucun de ceux-ci (ओकां द सअ सी) (None of these) (इनमें से कोई नहीं)
Clergé et noblesse (क्लेरज़े ए नॉबलेस) (Clergy and nobility) (पादरी और बड़प्पन)

5. 'The Spirit of Laws' est écrit par ? ('स्पिरिट ऑफ लॉज' ए एकृत पा ?) ('The Spirit of Laws' is written by?) ('स्पिरिट ऑफ लॉज' किसके द्वारा लिखा गया है?)
Abbe Sleyes (अब्बे स्लीयस)
Montesquleu (मोंटेस्क्ल्यू)
Rousseau (रूसो)
Aucun de ceux-ci (ओकां द सअ-सी)

6. Le livre qui proposait une division du pouvoir au sein du gouvernement? (ल लिव्र की प्रोपोसे इयुन दिविज़ियो दू पुवुआर ओ सां दू गवर्न्मों ?) (The book that proposed a division of power within the government?) (वह पुस्तक जिसने सरकार के भीतर सत्ता के विभाजन का प्रस्ताव रखा था?)
Two Treaties of Government (टू ट्रीटाइज ऑफ गवर्नमेंट)
The Spirit of the Laws (द स्पिरिट ऑफ द लॉ)
Le Moniteur Universal (ल मॉनिटर यूनिवर्सल)
The Social Contract (द सोशल कॉन्ट्रैक्ट)

7. Qui était le roi de France au moment de la Révolution ? (की एते ल रुआ द फ्रॉन्स ओ मोमो द ला रेवोलुसियो ?) (Who was the King of France at the time of the Revolution?) (क्रांति के समय फ्रांस का राजा कौन था?)
Louis XIV (लुई XIV)
Louis XVI (लुई XVI)
James (जेम्स)
Nicholas II (निकोलस II)

8. Le patron du Jacobin Club ? (ला पात्रों दू जैकोबिन क्लब ?) (The head of Jacobin Club?) (जैकोबिन क्लब के प्रमुख?)
Maximilian Robesplerre (मैक्सिमिलियन रोबेस्प्लेरे)
Louis XVI (लुई XVI)
Nicholas II (निकोलस II)
Montesquleu (मोंटेस्क्ल्यू)

9. Quel événement est le plus étroitement associé à la Révolution française ? (केल एवेन्मो ए ल प्लु ऐतरुआत असोसियो आ ला रेवोलुसियो फ्रांसेज़ ?) (Which event is most closely associated with the French Revolution?) (कौन सी घटना फ्रांसीसी क्रांति से सबसे अधिक निकटता से जुड़ी हुई है?)
Concile de Trente (कोंसिल द त्रोंत) (Council of Trent) (ट्रेंट की परिषद)
Guerre de Trente ans (गैर द त्रोंत ऑ) (Thirty years War) (तीस साल का युद्ध)
Règne de terreur (रैन द तेर) (Reign of Terror) (आतंक का शासनकाल)
Aucun de ceux-ci (ओकां द सअ-सी) (None of these) (इनमें से कोई नहीं)

10. Qui a écrit le livre « Two Treaties of the Govermnent » ? (की आ एकृत ल लिव्र « टू ट्रीटीज ऑफ द गवर्नमेंट » ?)

(Who wrote the book “Two Treaties of the Government”?) (“टू ट्रीटीज ऑफ द गवर्नमेंट” पुस्तक किसने लिखी है?)
John Locke (जॉन लॉक)
Louis XVI (लुई XVI)
Nicholas II (निकोलस II)
Montesquleu (मोंटेस्क्ल्यू)

Answer: 1-a, 2-c, 3-c, 4-d, 5-b, 6-b, 7-b, 8-a, 9-c, 10-a.

Exercise 44: Reliez les mots Suivant. (रलिये ले मो सुअिवांत।) (Match the following words.) (निम्नलिखित शब्दों का मिलान करें।)

FRENCH
1. Guerre (गैर)
2. Davantage (दावोंताज़)
3. Inconnu (आंकोनु)
4. Acheter (आशते)
5. Droits (दरुआत)
6. Réintroduire (रियात्रोदुइ)
7. Porter (पोर्ते)
8. Liberté (लिबर्ते)
9. Bientôt (बिआंतो)
10. Esclave (एसकलाव)

ENGLISH
a. Further (आगे)
b. Unfamiliar (अपरिचित)
c. Wear (पहनें)
d. War (युद्ध)
e. Freedom (आजादी)
f. Rights (अधिकार)
g. Slave (गुलाम)
h. Buy (खरीदें)

Answer: 1-d, 2-a, 3-b, 4-h, 5-f, 6-j, 7-c, 8-e, 9-i, 10-g

Exercise 45: Remplir les espaces vides. (रांपलीर लेज़ैसपास वीदा) (Fill in the Blanks.) (रिक्त स्थान भरो।)

1. Au matin du ______, la ville de Paris est en état d'alerte. (औ मातां दू _______, ला विल द पारी ए ऑ एता दालेर्त।) (On the morning of, ______, the city of Paris was in a state of alarm.) (_______, की सुबह, पेरिस शहर खतरे की स्थिति में था।)

2. La _____ est l'hymne national de la France composé par le poète Roget de L'Isle. (ला _____ ए लिम नासियोनाल द ला फ्रान्स कंपोज़े पा ल पोएत रोजेट डी ल'इस्ले।) (The _____ is the national anthem of France composed by the poet Roget de L’Isle.) (फ्रांस का राष्ट्रगान _____ है जिसकी रचना कवि रोजेट डी ल आइल ने की है।)

3. Louis XVI a été exécuté publiquement sur la____. (लुई XVI आ एते एजेकुते पुब्लिकमों सुर ला____।) (Louis XVI was executed publicly at the ____.) (लुई सोलहवें को ____ में सार्वजनिक रूप से मार डाला गया था।)

4. ______a rédigé une Déclaration des droits de la femme et du citoyen. (______आ रेदिजे इयुन देक्लेरसियो द दरुआ द ला फाम ए दू सीतोया।) (______wrote a Declaration of the Rights of Woman and Citizen.) (______ने महिलाओं और नागरिकों के अधिकारों की घोषणा लिखी।)

5. La traite des esclaves a commencé au____ siècle. (ले त्रेते द एस्कालाव अ कोमोंसे ओ ____ सीएक्ल।) (The slave trade began in the ____ century.) (गुलामों का व्यापार ____ शताब्दी में शुरू हुआ।)

6. La charge du financement des activités de l'État par l'impôt était supportée par le seul ____état. (ला शार्ज दू फिनोस्मो देस आक्तिविते द लेता पा लाम्पो एते सपोरते प् ल सल ____एता।) (The burden of financing activities of the state through taxes was borne by the ____estate alone.) (करों के माध्यम से राज्य की वित्तीय गतिविधियों का बोझ अकेले ____एस्टेट द्वारा वहन किया गया था।)

7. _____a été condamné à mort par un tribunal pour trahison. (____ आ एते कोंदाने आ मोर् पा अं त्रिबुनाल पूर त्राऐज़ो।) (____ was sentenced to death by a court on the charge of treason.) (____ को एक अदालत ने राजद्रोह के आरोप में मौत की सजा सुनाई थी।)

8. _____a proposé une forme de gouvernement basée sur un contrat social entre le peuple et ses représentants. (_____आ प्रोपोज़े इयुन फ्रॉर्म द ग्वेर्नमो बासे सुर अं कंत्रात सोसिआल आंत्र ल पुपल ए से रेप्रेसेंतों।) (_____ proposed a form of government based on a social contract between people and their representatives.) (_____ ने लोगों और उनके प्रतिनिधियों के बीच एक सामाजिक अनुबंध के आधार पर सरकार के एक रूप का प्रस्ताव रखा।)

9. _____a cherché à réfuter la doctrine du droit divin et absolu du monarque. (_____ आ शरशे आ रेफूते ला दोंक्त्रिन दू दरुआ दिवां ए ऑब्सलू दू मोनार्क।) (_____ sought to refute the doctrine of the divine and absolute right of the Monarch.) (_____ ने सम्राट के दैवीय और पूर्ण अधिकार के सिद्धांत का खंडन करने की मांग की।)

10. Les____sont connus sous le nom de sans-culottes. (ल _____ सों कोनू सौं ल नोम द सँ-कुलोत।) (_____came to be known as the sans-culottes.) (_____ को सेन्य अपराधी के रूप में जाना जाने लगा।)

(Answer: 1-14 Juillet (जुलिए) (July) (जुलाई),1789
2-Marseillaise (मार्सिलेज़)
3-Place de la Concorde (प्लेस डे ला कॉनकॉर्ड)
4-Olympe de Gouges (ओलम्पे डी गौगेस)
5- Dix-septième (सत्रहवाँ)
6-Tiers (तीसरा)
7- Louis XVI (लुई XVI)
8-Rousseau (रूसो)
9-Locke (लॉक)
10-Jacobins (जेकोबीन)

Exercise 46: Réponse en un mot. (रेपॉन्स औ आं मो।) (One word answer.) (एक शब्द का उत्तर।)

1. Quand la Révolution française a-t-elle éclaté ? (कौ ल रेवोलुसिओं फ्राँसे अ-तेलेक्लाते ?) (When did the French Revolution break?) (फ्रांसीसी क्रांति कब टूट गई?)

2. Quand la France est-elle devenue une monarchie constitutionnelle ? (कौ ल फ्रांस एत एल दवेन्यु इयुन मोनार्शी कॉन्स्टिट्यूशन ?) (When did the France become constitutional monarchy?) (फ्रांस संवैधानिक राजतंत्र कब बना?)

3. Quelle forme de gouvernement était en pratique en France en 1789 ? (कैल फॉर्म द गवेर्नमो एते ऑ प्रातिक ऑन फ्रांस ऑन 1789 ?) (What from of government was in practice in France in 1789?) (1789 में फ्रांस में सरकार की ओर से क्या चलन में था?)

4. Nommez l'impôt qui a été payé directement à l'état en France ? (नोमे लाम्पो की आ एते पेये दिरेक्ट्मों लेता ऑन फ्रांस ?) (Name the tax which was paid directly to the state in France?) (उस कर का नाम बताइए जो फ्रांस में राज्य को सीधे भुगतान किया जाता था?)

5. Qui était le souverain de la France en 1789 ? (की एत ल सयुवरा द ला फ्रांस ऑन 1789 ?) (Who was the ruler of France in 1789?) (1789 में फ्रांस का शासक कौन था?)

6. Que signifie un sceptre ? (क सिनिफिए अं सेपत् ?) (What does a sceptre stand for?) (राजदंड का क्या अर्थ है?)

7. Qui était le vaincu dans la bataille de Waterloo ? (की एते ल वैंक्यु दौ ला बाताई द वातरलू ?) (Who was the defeated in the battle of waterloo?) (वाटरलू के युद्ध में कौन पराजित हुआ था?)

8. Qui a écrit l'esprit des lois ? (की आ एक्रित लासप्रीत दे लुआ ?) (Who wrote the spirite of the laws?) (द स्पिरिट ऑफ द लॉज किसने लिखा है?)

Answer: 1-14 Juillet (जुलिए) (July) (जुलाई),1789, 2-1791, 3-Monarchie (मोनार्शी), 4-Taille (टाइल), 5-Louis XVI (लुई XVI), 6-Symbole du pouvoir royal (साम्बोल दू पुवुआ रोयॉल), 7-Napoléon (नेपोलियन), 8-Montesquieu (मोंटेस्क्ल्यू)

Exercise 47: Dites vrai/faux. (दित व्रे/फो।) (Say true/false.) (सही/गलत बताओ।)

1. Louis XVI monta sur le trône le 12 mai 1774. (लुइ XVI मोंता सुर ल त्रोन ल 12 मै 1774.) (Louis XVI ascended the throne in the year 12th May, 1774.) (लुई सोलहवें 12 मई, वर्ष 1774 में गद्दी पर बैठा।)

2. La traite des esclaves a commencé au XVIIe siècle. (ले त्रेते द एस्कालाव अ कोमोंसे ओ XVIIe सीएक्ल।) (The slave trade began in the seventeenth century.) (गुलामों का व्यापार सत्रहवीं शताब्दी में शुरू हुआ।)

3. Louis XVI a été condamné à mort par un tribunal pour avoir voté. (लुइ XVI आ एते कोंदाने मोर् पा अं त्रिबुनाल पूर अवुआर वोते।) (Louis XVI was sentenced to death by a court on the charge of voting.) (लुई सोलहवें को एक अदालत ने वोटिंग के आरोप में मौत की सजा सुनाई थी।)

4. L'action de trahir son pays ou un gouvernement est connue sous le nom de trahison. (लेक्सीओं द त्राहिर सौ पेइ उ अं गवेर्नमो ए कोनू सू ल नॉम द त्राहीसों।) (The action of betraying one's country or a government is known as Treason.) (किसी के देश या सरकार को धोखा देने की कार्रवाई को देशद्रोह के रूप में जाना जाता है।)

5. En 1804, Népoléon se couronne empereur de France. (ऑन 1804, नेपोलियन स कुरो ओमपर्र द फ्रॉन्स।) (In 1804, Nepoleon crowned himself Emperor of France.) (1804 में, नेपोलियन ने खुद को फ्रांस का सम्राट घोषित किया।)

6. L'idée de liberté et les droits démocratiques ont été l'héritage le plus important de la Révolution française.
(लीदे द लिबर्ते ए ल दरुआ डेमोक्रेटिक ऑ एते लेरिताज़ ल प्लु आम्पोर्त द ला रेवोलुसिओं फ्रांसे।) (The Idea of liberty and democratic rights were the most important legacy of the France Revolution.) (स्वतंत्रता और लोकतांत्रिक अधिकारों का विचार फ्रांस क्रांति की सबसे महत्वपूर्ण विरासत थी।)

7. La société française était divisée en Trois Domaines. (ल सोसियतें फ्रांसे एते दिविज़े ऑ त्रुआ दोमैन।) (French society was divided into three estate.) (फ्रांसीसी समाज तीन सम्पदा में विभाजित किया गया था।)

8. 'The Spirit of Laws' est écrit par Abbe Sleyes. ('स्पिरिट ऑफ लॉज' ए एकृत पा अब्बे स्लीयस।) ('The Spirit of Laws' is written by Abbe Sleyes.) ('स्पिरिट ऑफ लॉज' अब्बे स्लीयस द्वारा लिखा गया है।)

9. 'Prise de la Bastille' s'est produit 14 juillet 1777. ('परीज़ द ला बास्ति' से प्रोदुई 14 जुलिए 1777.) ('Storming of the Bastille' occured on 14 july 1777.) ('स्टॉर्मिंग ऑफ द बैस्टिल' 14 जुलाई 1777 हुआ था।)

10. Le patron du Jacobin Club était Maximilian Robesplerre. (ला पात्रों दू जैकोबिन क्लब एते मैक्सिमिलियन रोबेस्प्लेरे।) (The head of Jacobin Club was Maximilian Robesplerre.) (जैकोबिन क्लब के प्रमुख मैक्सिमिलियन रोबेस्प्लेरे था।)

Answer: 1-faux, 2-vrai, 3-faux, 4-vrai, 5-vrai, 6-vrai, 7-vrai, 8-faux, 9-faux, 10-vrai